THE CORPORATE TRAINER'S QUICK REFERENCE

Geoffrey Moss

BUSINESS ONE IRWIN
Homewood, Illinois 60430

Previously published by Moss Associates Ltd., New Zealand, as *The Trainer's Handbook*. Also published in New Zealand by the Ministry of Agriculture and Fisheries, in Australia by CCH Australia Ltd., and in Singapore by the Singapore Institute of Management. First published in Great Britain as *The Trainer's Desk Reference* by Kogan Page in 1991. This is a 1992 revised edition.
© RICHARD D. IRWIN, INC., 1993

Sponsoring editor: Cynthia A. Zigmund
Project editor: Jess Ann Ramirez
Production manager: Diane Palmer
Jacket designer: Michael Finkelman
Compositor: TCSystems, Inc.
Typeface: 10/11 Helvetica
Printer: Book Press, Inc.

Library of Congress Cataloging-in-Publication Data

Moss, Geoffrey, date
    The corporate trainer's quick reference/Geoffrey Moss.—1992
rev. ed.
        p.   cm.
    Originally published: The trainer's desk reference. Great Britain
Kogan Page, 1991.
    Includes index.
    ISBN 1-55623-905-X
    1. Employees—Training of —Handbooks, manuals, etc.   I. Moss,
Geoffrey, date Trainer's desk reference.   II. Title.
HF5549.5.T7M68   1993
658.3′ 124—dc20   92–34937

Printed in the United States of America
1 2 3 4 5 6 7 8 9 0 BP 9 8 7 6 5 4 3

Dedicated to Robyn, Graeme, Lynette, and David, all good teachers and trainers.

One must learn by doing things;
for though you think you know it
you have no certainty, until you try.

Sophocles, *496–406* B.C.

Preface

Perhaps this book should have been called *Training by Participation.* That's what training today is all about—involving learners in their own training by having them set their own goals, actively participate in training sessions, and share experiences.

The aim of training should be to inspire action rather than fill the trainee with knowledge soon forgotten. The important and successful people in this world, the achievers, are those who inspire people and get things done.

This book was written to help new trainers get started and also to help managers understand the benefits of training. Managers can change an organization if they treat training as an investment. There can be good returns if training is relevant and meets the needs of the organization. Remember—training is for the future.

This book will show new trainers how to plan and start training and how to estimate returns on training. It is full of hints from top international trainers and should help you avoid many costly mistakes.

Most training books are large, encyclopedic, and full of jargon. My aim is to explain training in simple terms. I have tried to get rid of training gobbledygook and to get down to the basic principles with simplified concepts, summaries, and checklists. But I have also tried to show that training should be challenging and fun, using a variety of techniques and involving the trainees as much as possible.

I hope readers will find this a user-friendly book. The table of contents gives a detailed list of the contents of each chapter, and there is a comprehensive index. The catalog of training techniques in Chapter 8 and the visual aids in Chapter 9 have been listed in alphabetical order for ease of reference.

Electronic technology has added new dimensions to training. The increased use of teleconferences, video conferences, and computer-assisted learning can make training more challenging and enjoyable. You can now bring world authorities into your training rooms with a minimum of effort. But don't get carried away with the tools of training—it's the basic objectives, work skills, and motivation that are more important. Get the basics right—you will be well rewarded!

Geoffrey Moss

All knowledge is sterile which does not lead to action.

Mercier

Acknowledgments

My grateful thanks to all my friends and colleagues from many countries who have shared their training ideas with me.

Special thanks to Joyce Moss as editor.

G. M.

Contents

Chapter One

Why Train?

Let's face it: the only constant thing in business today is change.

For organizations to survive, managers need to increase efficiency and reduce costs. This is often done by reducing staff numbers and giving remaining staff greater responsibility.

Organizations are only as good as their employees and if managers want good employees they have two choices: hire or train.

Training isn't a quick fix—it's a budgeted item like research and development.

Training should be planned to meet corporate goals and objectives. Therefore it is essential for trainers to have a close working relationship with top management.

IT'S A GROWTH SITUATION

Each one of us will have to be retrained many times in our careers or we will be replaced.

An organization is like a tree; as it grows, it produces new branches and more leaves to sustain its growth. If an organization stands still, it doesn't survive.

You can change a whole organization with an enlightened training policy. But training must be treated as a development process rather than as a series of isolated events.

THE WEAKNESS OF FORMAL TRAINING

Far too often, training fails because workers who are taken off the job to attend a formal course think it is a punishment for their own inadequacies and they resist the training. How are you going to change this attitude?

It takes more than a short course to change habits that are the results of years of reinforcement.

'Tis harder to unlearn than learn.

Proverb

USE CHALLENGING ASSIGNMENTS

Workers should be rotated into challenging assignments. This is a good way to stimulate personal growth, particularly if you use mentors to counsel and advise. Get employees involved with their training. Let them try out new things even if they make mistakes at first.

We rarely learn from our successes but we learn from our mistakes.

TARGET KEY AREAS

Target training at areas where good results will benefit the organization and give good returns.

Look for areas where new technology, new procedures, or new policies have created changes. These will be your high pay-off training areas.

Focus training on a few key concepts—don't overtrain or give too many details. But if you are teaching a new skill, give practice, practice, and more practice.

INVOLVE SUPERVISORS IN TRAINING

Supervisors should be involved in helping to plan and carry out training. Without their commitment, support, and encouragement, training can be wasted.

MONITOR PROGRESS

All training should be evaluated by the trainer, by the trainees, and by the manager.

Your aim is to assess the strengths and weaknesses of the training activity. You want feedback and suggestions for improvements. The evaluations may be ongoing, carried out at the end of training, or sometime after it is completed.

As a trainer, you must be objective about the exercise. You can improve only if you get honest feedback.

When trainees return to work, their supervisors should monitor their progress regularly. This is a good time for coaching and sympathetic counseling.

Support and encouragement are essential as a follow-up to all training, especially when new skills have been taught.

Feedback is the key to improvement.

RETURN ON INVESTMENT

As a trainer, you must never forget you are working for management, *not* for your trainees.

You must convince your managers they are getting good value for the money they are allocating for training.

How are you going to convince them your training budget is a sound investment?

- Prepare your training objectives to help achieve organizational goals and objectives.
- Build your training programs to meet needs.
- Observe and document gains in skills, knowledge, and attitudes after training.
- Estimate returns on training. (When you do your budget, don't forget to allow for time off from work during training—it's often the biggest cost.)
- Keep within your training budget.

Returns from learning should be more earnings.

IS TRAINING A GOOD INVESTMENT?

Your managers will want to know whether your training is helping the organization grow. Try to estimate returns on training.

Do a few simple calculations to find the annual costs and earnings of the workers and the amount spent on training.

As a starting point, go back over annual reports and talk to the finance and personnel managers in your organization.

- Find out what each employee costs the organization. Calculate the total amount spent on wages, benefits, and taxes. Divide this amount by the number of staff.
- Go back over several years and graph the trends. If possible, get estimates and information to help you project your graph into the future.
- Try breaking down these figures into departments and types of jobs to see if you can discover any significant differences.
- Next, calculate what each person earns for the organization. Divide the total profits by the number of staff.
- Again, repeat this calculation for several previous years and graph the trends. If possible, project your graph into the future.
- Find out the total value of assets per employee. Divide the total value of facilities and equipment by the number of employees.

This will give you the value of the facilities and equipment that the average employee is responsible for using or maintaining. Some machines and equipment need operators with greater skills and knowledge, and more training is required.

- What is the average amount spent on each employee for training and development? Consider different jobs in the organization and calculate how much is spent on training the different categories of workers.
- Is the money being spent in areas of greatest return?
- Is sufficient money being spent on training?

What does it cost to train?
But what does it cost NOT to train?

YOUR CHALLENGE

Your job is to prove to management that the training budget is being spent in support of management goals and objectives.

- Is the training budget being used to help
  Increase production?
  Increase profits?
  Improve quality?
  Reduce staff turnover?
  Reduce accidents?
  Reduce lost time?
  Improve morale?
  Improve client satisfaction?
  Improve the public image of the organization?

Your job is to prove it is. That's your challenge!

Such information will give you baselines to start measuring training effectiveness. It will help you locate priority areas for training and give you figures to present to management to build a case for an adequate training budget.

Increased profits come from training better staff and having fewer of them.

Chapter Two

The Learning Process

After You Have Read This Chapter, You Should Be Able To:

List Some Important Principles of Learning

Make Your Training More Effective When Teaching Adults

LEARNING IS PERSONAL

Learning is a very personal process. It is an active process—not the "pouring" in of messages. The learner reacts to the message and the learning brings about a change in behavior, be it mental, emotional, or physical. It can also be stressful.

CONDUCIVE CONDITIONS

Managers and trainers can do much to stimulate and encourage learning by selecting methods that will provide the experiences that promote learning. They should aim also for physical and mental climates that will be conducive to learning.

COMFORT ASSISTS LEARNING

We learn best when we are comfortably at ease, without too many distractions.

This physical comfort is much more important than most people realize. A "schoolroom" situation is often not conducive to adult learning, especially if the memories of school-day learning are not particularly happy ones. Remember that most of the factors that inhibit learning are self-imposed by the learner.

ADAPT TEACHING TO NEEDS

The "psychological climate" can be manipulated in various ways. The teaching should be adapted to the needs and language of your audience—to the speed of their learning and to their previously acquired knowledge. Try to make trainees feel at ease. Make them feel they know something and can contribute. Examine the individual differences of opinion and strive not to embarrass any of the trainees. Help them to see they can disagree without being disagreeable.

SOME IMPORTANT PRINCIPLES OF LEARNING

Involvement

We are more likely to remember a solution we have worked out for ourselves than one that has been thought out for us—also to act on the decisions we have made for ourselves rather than on those that have been made for us.

Readiness

Learning will take place more quickly if we want to learn and are ready to learn.

Reinforcement

Repetition and meaningful exercises in a nonhostile environment will overcome "interference" from other learning.

Intensity

Intense, dramatic, or vivid experiences are likely to make an impression by capturing the attention and strengthening the impact.

Association

Learning that is related to our own experiences (so similarities and differences can be seen) is more likely to be remembered.

Distribution

Learning distributed over several short lessons is more effective than if it is crammed into a single, long lesson.

Effectiveness

Learning is more likely to occur when it is satisfying than when it is embarrassing or annoying. Approval encourages learning.

Capacity

Most of us remain at a stage that is far below our real capacity for learning, working, and achieving.

DRAWING ON COMBINED EXPERIENCES

Often I have worked with groups whose total years of experience in the topic under discussion have added up to several hundreds. How can any tutor with, say, 25 years' experience hope to match the combined experience of such a group? Good tutors do not try to do so. Rather they seek to "cash in" on other people's experiences and to tap this knowledge by leading a discussion along planned lines. Adults learn well when they are sharing experiences. Very often they will relate better to one another than to the professional, who frequently lacks practical experience in the topic.

The professional tutor, teacher, or extension worker has (or should have) the skills to define a problem; to decide on objectives; and to draw people out, so that they share their experiences and thus work toward a planned goal.

At the same time, the tutor needs to be firm enough to know when to interrupt people who digress or who start to monopolize a discussion. Like the good chairman, a good tutor needs to keep one eye on the clock, for time usually needs to be rationed.

EVERYBODY HAS COMMITMENTS

Everyday pressures at home can cause adults to "turn off" for periods that break the concentration necessary for effective learning.

An adult's learning is interwoven with many other activities and responsibilities. Younger persons, with fewer responsibilities, usually have more time to concentrate on learning.

There are advantages in running a course in a residential center away from home and work environments. You take the members away from their daily responsibilities. If you can keep them fully occupied with work and social activities, you will see greater concentration given to your discussion topics.

NEW TRICKS FOR OLD DOGS

Research has dispelled the myth that an old dog cannot be taught new tricks.

Increasing age does affect one's performance speed and reaction time. The result? We absorb learning at a somewhat slower rate. This does not mean any lessening of the *ability* to learn. Many people, in all fields of creative endeavor, make their biggest contributions in later life.

But, because the learning *rate* for adults does tend to be slower, the lessons must be "hammered home" by repetition, by examples, and by demonstrations.

OUR DECLINING FACULTIES

An adult's vision usually changes rapidly between 40 and 50 years of age. Hearing and physical reactions also decline. We are, however, often loath to acknowledge our physical failings and defects. The tutor needs to be aware of these difficulties and must ensure that everybody can hear and see adequately.

- Make sure your visual aids are really "visible."

- Check that the acoustics are adequate.

- Try to shut out any interfering noises.

- Encourage clear, distinct speech.

HOW WE LEARN

FIGURE 1

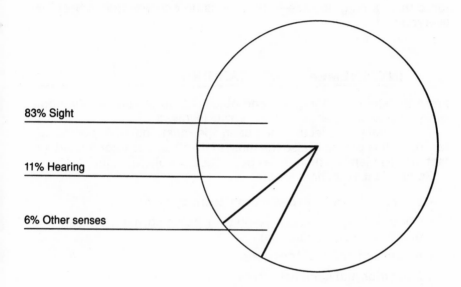

83% Sight

11% Hearing

6% Other senses

ADULTS VARY ENORMOUSLY

The tutor should always know as much as possible about the needs and the knowledge level of each of the students before planning any training program.

Adults, like children, learn at varying speeds. There are thus advantages in having a variety of training tools in your training kit. Each of them will suit some people better than others.

VARIETY IN METHODS

People of all ages learn more rapidly from a variety of teaching methods than from a single one.

In general, we learn best from actually doing a job, next best from what we see, then from what we read and hear. A lecture is an ineffective way of teaching—but if it is used in conjunction with other techniques, its effectiveness can be increased. The spoken word should be reinforced with visual aids, demonstrations, and handouts.

Whenever possible, repetition in a nonthreatening environment is a valuable way to learn a new skill.

A variety of teaching techniques is perhaps the best way to reinforce the learning process—but there is no one way that is best for everybody.

INVOLVEMENT AIDS LEARNING

From the setting of the goals and objectives to the final evaluation, every course member should be heavily involved.

Traditionally, the lecture has been the most common method of teaching. It is probably also the most ineffective. The tutor should, in fact, use as many techniques as possible to involve the students.

Some of these techniques are:

- Direct, purposeful experiences ("learn by doing").
- Contrived experiences (role-playing, debating, initiative tests, demonstrations, exercises).
- Group and paired discussions.
- Field trips and demonstrations.
- Forums and panel discussions.
- TV, videos, and films.

We learn best when we are enjoying our learning—when we are being challenged and entertained by a variety of exercises and competitions.

AVOID RIDICULE

The adult places a high value on the goodwill and approval of friends, neighbors, family, and colleagues at work. We fear ridicule, but we fear being shut out from the companionship of others even more. The most progressive and innovating adults have confidence in their own judgment and have less need for the approval of others.

Adults resent being pushed around and told what to do. We all want to be respected, intelligent, responsible human beings. We can accept help and advice only when doing so does not challenge our self-respect or our integrity as a person.

FIGURE 2
The Value of Various Aids to Learning

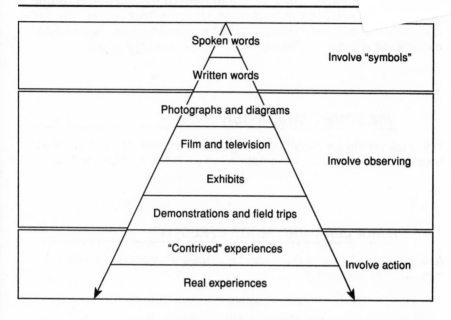

Spoken words

Written words

Involve "symbols"

Photographs and diagrams

Film and television

Exhibits

Involve observing

Demonstrations and field trips

"Contrived" experiences

Real experiences

Involve action

- Words are least effective "teaching aid".
- Real experiences are the most effective.

Be careful, too, not to violate the status and self-respect of your students, their satisfaction in their work, or their social environment. Never embarrass senior staff in front of juniors, or vice versa.

Be sensitive to racial and sexual differences. If they become a problem, discuss them openly.

TEACH JUST A LITTLE

When you are trying to bring about change, don't be in a hurry. Take time to listen before you start to introduce your new ideas. It is better to teach just a little and teach it well rather than pour words over people ineffectively.

AROUSE INTEREST BEFORE YOU START

We learn more easily when we are interested in the subject. Confidence and knowledge make us more receptive to learning. You will often find that a new skill will be picked up rapidly by persons who can already see when and where they will find a use for it.

USE YOUR IMAGINATION

Don't take traditional methods for granted. Experiment with different training ways. Use your imagination—it's a powerful training tool.

MAKE LEARNING MORE EFFECTIVE

Anyone who wishes to learn can be helped to improve the effectiveness of their learning.

- Work hard at maintaining attention and interest.
- Promote the recall of previously learned material.
- Break down large concepts into small learning units.
- Give continuous progress reports and encouragement.
- Allow sufficient practice time for becoming familiar with recently acquired skills and knowledge.
- Keep all your teaching material up to date and relevant.

COPING WITH IMPATIENCE

Learning new skills takes time. In many cases, constant practice over a long period may be required (learning how to be a good public speaker or a writer is likely to take years of practice). However, many students become frustrated when results do not come quickly.

Often the tutor has been to blame for setting unrealistic goals. To set an objective such as "to teach management skills" and then to expect to produce a whole set of managers by bringing people together for one brief residential course would be ludicrous.

SIGNPOSTS AND MILEAGE CHECKS

A good way to start a training course is to discuss objectives—what both tutor and students are hoping to gain. This will help to establish realistic goals.

A good training course can be compared to a car journey. There should be a prearranged destination, adequate signposting, and regular map and mileage checks to make sure where you are and whether you're on the right road. Unfortunately, many tutors become overcommitted or do not have sufficient support services available. They need to be able to arrange adequate maintenance checks and repairs and for a sufficient fuel supply to keep the vehicle moving at a safe speed, allowing the passengers time to enjoy the scenery on the way.

As the training proceeds, you should be making regular evaluations and progress reports.

A "course evaluation" at the end of the course is of little use to the students. Regular checks should be made throughout. They provide a gauge as to the relevance and the effectiveness of the techniques that are being used—and a chance to change the course content, if necessary.

Nothing will sustain the adult in learning more than the feeling of "getting somewhere." Nothing is more frustrating than the absence of feedback or any indication of progress. Evaluations are important. A sense of achievement is one of our most satisfying experiences—especially achievement in learning.

AFTER IT'S ALL OVER

People often have difficulty in readjusting to their jobs after a period of refresher study. This is caused by the difficulty of relating what they have learned with what they are required to do. They may also have to contend with resentment from their colleagues who were not given the chance to attend the course.

Often, the adult learner who has been to such a course has been stimulated into trying to bring about changes too rapidly. This causes resentment, so that the new methods are resisted. This is very common when someone has been fired with enthusiasm after a period of study overseas.

A discussion on such problems at the conclusion of a training period can be well worthwhile.

What we have to learn to do, we learn by doing.

Aristotle

Chapter Three

So You Want to Be a Successful Trainer

After You Have Read This Chapter, You Should Be Able to Plan to Be a More Successful Trainer

QUESTION, PLAN, INVOLVE

- Why were you the successful applicant for your job?
- What does your boss expect of you?
- Read your job description. What is needed to satisfy its requirements?
- What are the standards for judging your performance?
- What are your strengths? Do you make the most of them?

Have regular discussions with key senior staff—they have the authority to make use of what you are teaching.

Look for the successes and failures of previous training sessions—find out the reasons for some of them.

Be ready to discuss people's problems as they see them. This is most important.

Concentrate on high-return areas—establish your credibility by selecting training projects that you know will be successful.

Follow up early successes to ensure they are fully exploited.

Your continuing success will depend on your being able to help management to reach its objectives—it is therefore essential for you to know at all times what those objectives are.

You must have direct communication with top management at all times.

Establish a regular feedback from all training activities. Evaluate regularly—never wait until the end of an exercise or course.

Be flexible and learn to profit from helpful criticism.

At the end of every training course, assess what you have achieved.

It is often hard to get honest "face-to-face" comments. Ask participants to complete a reaction evaluation form at the end of training or carry out a postal evaluation after they return home.

HELPFUL HINTS

- Every person in every group is unique, with a different background and learning needs.
- Every training program needs to be planned and developed to suit the varied needs of the group members.
- Assess the general standard of learning and knowledge so that you can begin at an appropriate level.
- Start with a topic that is familiar to the group, but add something new to stimulate curiosity and to arouse awareness of previously unrecognized needs.
- Move forward one step at a time.
- Adjust the size and difficulty of each step to the learners' abilities.
- Be prepared to adjust each step, not only to the group as a whole but to any individual in the group—determine their readiness to learn, their familiarity with what has to be learned, and their speed of learning.
- Build each step on the preceding step—relate later learning experiences to earlier ones.
- Make sure you provide opportunities for all members to practice their newly acquired skills.
- Relate everything to a "real-life" situation to show its meaning and application, and the variety of situations in which it can be used.
- Paint a clear picture of any changes you are attempting to make—explain the reasons for change.
- Be flexible in all your methods—if you really "have your finger on the pulse" of the group, you should be able to feel when it is ready for a new learning experience.
- Try to put yourself in the other person's shoes and to imagine how you would feel, react, and behave if you were the person being trained.
- Try always to be tolerant and understanding.

- Encouragement and praise are among the cheapest and best of all training tools—they are also among the least used.
- Every course must have its clear objectives and expectations— the terms must have the same meaning for everyone.
- Remember that meanings are in people's minds—not in the words themselves.
- Keep your students hard at work for limited periods only— never for indefinite, unspecified stretches. Allow enough time for creative thinking to produce worthwhile ideas.
- Remember that lengthy periods of physical inactivity in the confines of a room do not usually encourage creative thinking. Set deadlines and try to keep to them.
- Imagination can play an important role in learning. ("Suppose you had just been made president; what would you do. . . ?")
- Try to make every member feel "involved"—to feel they can share experiences freely, without fear of "losing face."
- Exercises should be seen to be worthwhile and relevant— preferably ending with useful, practicable recommendations.
- Develop a working climate that encourages constructive self-criticism. ("How can I do better next time?")
- Regular evaluations will help to build great empathy among the course members and will allow for any changes in direction that may become necessary.
- Involve everyone in experience sharing, but make sure comments are concise so that everybody has a chance to participate.
- Don't forget that the traditional lecture is probably the most ineffective way to teach.
- Real experiences are the most effective.
- Words are the least effective teaching aid.

AIM FOR ACTION

Training programs need careful planning and preparation if they are to be successful.

There are 11 main steps:

11	Review program and revise if necessary.
10	Evaluate.
9	Carry out training.
8	Decide how the program is to be evaluated.
7	Prepare lesson plans.
6	Select training techniques, methods, aids.
5	Select and organize the content of your program.
4	Set training objectives.
3	Assess the training needs.
2	Analyze the trainees.
1	Analyze the job.

Chapter Four

Planning Training

After You Have Read This Chapter, You Should Be Able To:

Analyze Your Trainees and Their Jobs

Identify Their Training Needs

Write Clear Training Objectives

Decide on Content of the Course

Select the Best Training Ways for Your Course

Prepare a Worksheet and Lesson Plan

Evaluate Your Training

There are three stages to successful training:

A. Detailed planning.

B. Adequate preparation.

C. Lively presentation.

Figure 3 outlines a training plan with the elements of the training process arranged in a logical sequence. If you work through these systematically, your training should be more effective. Remember that the more costly the training, the greater the effort you should put into the analysis and planning.

Any training plan should start with a good briefing from the initiator of the plan. Initiators are usually administrators or managers who set the goals to be achieved. They must be kept informed throughout the training because they are responsible for approving the training budget.

The first tasks are to analyze the job requirements, carry out a trainee analysis, and decide on their training needs. You are then able to determine the training objectives. See Figure 4.

FIGURE 3
Training Process

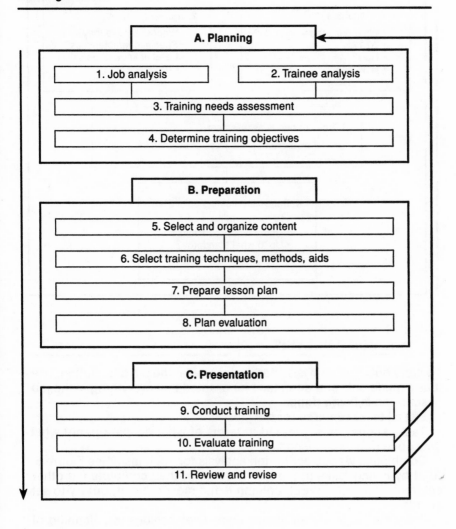

A. PLANNING THE TRAINING COURSE

FIGURE 4

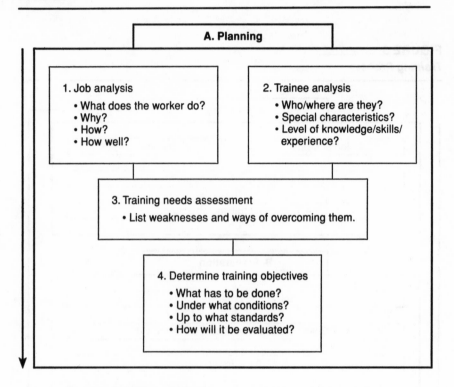

1. JOB ANALYSIS

To carry out a job analysis, start by looking at the job description. Use it as a guide only and don't take for granted that everything in the job description is being done.

List all tasks required for the job.

Tasks should be expressed in terms of what people do, **not** what gets done or accomplished.

Complete a worksheet for job analysis for each task. See Figure 5. Start by listing tasks in the WHAT column; then complete the other columns. The HOW WELL column is the most difficult, but try to set standards.

A completed job analysis has many uses besides the planning of training. It can be used as the basis for writing a manual, for counseling staff, or for reorganizing supervisory or work relationships.

FIGURE 5
Worksheet for Job Analysis (Separate Sheet for Each Task)

What Has to Be Done (Action Verb + Object)	Why (To Produce or Achieve What?)	How	How Well (What Is a Good Job?)
To.	In order to.	With whom?	Quantity
		Where?	Outputs required?
(See list of behavioral objective verbs, Figure 8)		Process or procedure	What results are needed?
		Using what tools/ equipment and facilities?	Quality: What standards are required?

2. TRAINEE ANALYSIS

Characteristics of Trainees that May Influence Your Training

1. *Physical characteristics:* Age and sex of trainees, size of group, location of training.
2. *Educational characteristics:* Language, vocabulary, knowledge, skills, learning style trainees are familiar with, etc.
3. *Psychological characteristics:* Prejudices, attitudes, beliefs, values, interests, motivation, norms, etc.
4. *Socioeconomic characteristics:* Status, occupation, authority.
5. *Working experiences:* On-the-job training, etc.

How Can You Collect This Information?

Interviews, questionnaires, group meetings, conversations, letters from trainees, interviews with colleagues, supervisors, etc.

Observation of trainees at work, tests, case studies, role-playing, reports, records of work, etc.

Usually a mixture of methods is best. Be tactful and gather only the information you need. Don't be too inquisitive. Figure 6 is a suggested guide for gathering data for a trainee analysis.

FIGURE 6
Data for Trainee Analysis

	Detailed Information		
Categories	*Essential*	*Useful*	*Not Necessary*
Education/training/experience			
Sex			
Age			
Occupation			
Affiliations/special interests/ aptitudes			
Knowledge of subject			
Language			
Attitudes, beliefs			
Authority			

Possible Headings for a Trainee Analysis Form

1. *Size* of group.
2. *Sex* ratio.
3. *Age* groups.
   a. 15–25.
   b. 26–35.
   c. 36–45.
   d. 46– .
4. *Location*—urban/rural (percentages).
5. *Education*—college, high school (percentages).
6. *Positions*—occupations.
7. *Years of experience* in present position.
8. Most *important tasks* trainees perform:
   1. _____
   2. _____
   3. _____
   4. _____

FIGURE 7
Trainee's Present Knowledge and Needs

Job Requirement	Trainee's Current Knowledge and Skills				
	Excellent	Good	Fair	Poor	Nil
1.					
2.					
3.					
4.					
Etc.					
Training Needs (evident from the above information)					
1.					
2.					
3.					
4.					
Etc.					

9. *Knowledge of trainees* about their work—good, fair, poor.

10. *Trainees' feelings and beliefs* about their job.

3. TRAINING NEEDS ASSESSMENT

When you have completed the job analysis and the trainee analysis, you should be able to assess their current knowledge and skills and so decide on their training needs. Figure 7 shows a suggested form to record these findings.

4. TRAINING OBJECTIVES

A training objective for a particular group is a target or an achievement. It should specify the type of change that is expected, when it will occur, and, finally, how it will be measured to determine its level of success.

In other words, it describes what trainees should be able to do at the end of their training that they could not do previously. Therefore,

FIGURE 8
Some Commonly Used Behavioral Objective Words

Choose	Determine	Explain	Practice
Classify	Differentiate	Identify	Prepare
Construct	Discuss	Indicate	Select
Define	Distinguish	Integrate	Specify
Describe	Establish	List	State
Designate	Evaluate	Name	Trace

trainee analysis and training needs assessment should be carried out well before training objectives are written.

An objective must:

Describe the final results.

Be specific and precise.

Describe a change that is measurable or observed (see Figure 8).

List criteria against which success can be measured or judged.

Mention all the essential conditions under which the results can be achieved.

Specify an end point.

ABCD on Writing Training Objectives

Before you start writing objectives, consider the following:

A. *Audience*—Who are you going to train? You should know the participants' or trainees' background.

B. *Behavior*—What type of change do you expect? You should be able to describe the desired change and explain its advantages.

C. *Condition*—When and under what conditions do you expect this change to occur? (e.g., "Improved performance should be evident after eight hours of demonstration and practice and a 40-minute lecture.")

D. *Degree*—How much change do you expect and how will you find out?

Example. Trainees, after one week's training in the applications of a computer software package, will be able to:

- Explain the capabilities of the package.
- Identify the specialized uses that can be adapted to the student's own problem-solving requirements.

- Prepare a spreadsheet using a client's own database, and solve any data-handling issues.
- Demonstrate clearly to new students all operating functions of the spreadsheet from COPY to FORMAT modes.
- Request feedback from the client and determine at the conclusion of training what functions need further clarification and follow-up.

B. PREPARATION FOR THE TRAINING COURSE

B. Preparation

5. Select and organize content

- Study sources of information.
- Decide on content.
- Organize content in logical sequence.

6. Select training techniques, methods, aids

- Decide on appropriate techniques.
- Select suitable methods.
- Decide on training aids required.

7. Prepare lesson plans

- Decide how each lesson is to be presented.
- Set out each lesson step by step.
- Allocate times for each activity.

8. Plan evaluation

- Decide on information required.
- Decide when this should be collected.
- Study methods of gathering information.
- Select method to be used.
- Prepare questions that have to be answered.

5. SELECT AND ORGANIZE CONTENT OF COURSE

After analyzing the training objectives, decide on the content of the course. This should cover the detailed knowledge, skills, and attitudes required on topics that support the objectives.

When selecting content:

Remember the purpose of the training.

Prepare an outline of the content.

Classify content into:
  a. *What must be known* (skills and knowledge that are essential to do the basic tasks).
  b. *What should be known* (skills and knowledge needed in order to perform additional or related tasks).
  c. *What could be known* (skills and knowledge that relate to the job but are not essential).

Build up a content selection worksheet. Figure 10 shows some suggested headings for this worksheet.

Organizing Content

The content should be put in logical order or sequence. Certain parts of the content will have to be understood before other subjects can be introduced. Logical order will produce faster learning.

Contents can be organized in different ways:

1. *Job peformance order.* Training is given in the order in which tasks are performed.

2. *Problem order.* Training is given in the order you would use to solve a problem.

3. *Simple to complex.* Training is given according to what the trainee needs to know before more complex ideas are introduced.

When the contents of the training course have been selected, classified, and arranged in suitable order, you can then decide on the training methods to use to make your training enjoyable and effective.

6. WHICH TRAINING METHODS SHOULD YOU USE?

To transfer knowledge, use:

Group discussions (questions and answers).
Group or individual exercises.

FIGURE 10
Content Selection Worksheet Objectives (Write Training Objective Here)

| | What Needs to Be Known | | | | | What Needs to Be Performed | | | |
Topic	Details	Must	Should	Could	Topic	Details	Must	Should	Could

Lectures (with handouts).
Forums.
Panel discussions.
Films, videos, etc.

To practice problem solving, use:

Case studies.
Brainstorming.
Discussion groups.
Exercises, etc.

To develop skills use:

Demonstrations for manual skills.
Role-playing for interpersonal skills.
Peer teaching.
Programmed instructions, etc.

To change attitudes, use:

Debates.
Displays.
Role-playing (for clarifying how others feel).
Group discussion (for group attitudes).
Individual exercises.
Demonstrations.
Campaigns, etc.

7. WORKSHEET AND LESSON PLAN

Lesson plans and worksheets should list the steps, activities, and equipment needed in training sessions. Before a lesson plan is written, the following questions should be answered:

Which training methods will be most suitable?
Which style of presentation is best?
How will new information be introduced?
Which audiovisual aids will be needed?

A lesson should be planned by writing an outline of what is to be taught and the methods to be used. Times should be allocated for the various activities. The places where training is to take place and all equipment needed should be checked also. Time should be allowed for summarizing the main points at the end of a lesson and also for distributing any necessary handouts.

Throughout all training, time should be allowed for monitoring progress and understanding by discussions, reviews, group exercises, and short tests/examinations.

Suggested headings for lesson preparation include:

Title.
Content.
Training ways.
Desired result from participants (knowledge, skill, attitudes).
Location, seating, etc.
Equipment and materials required (teaching aids.)
Time in training room.
Time on outside activities.

Suggested Lesson Plan

1. Review previous lessons.
2. Introduce the subject. Tell class the content of the lesson and desired results.
3. Lead in from previous training.
4. Obtain student involvement. Let them share their experiences.
5. Lecture with demonstrations, films, models, etc.
6. Student activity—visits, practicals, role-playing, debating.
7. Discussion or reports—arising from activities.
8. Summarize main points.
9. Outline next lesson plan.

A Checklist for Handouts

- First, get attention by explaining the importance of the content. Why should trainees read it? What's in it for them?
- Are the objectives stated in behavioral terms—stressing skills the reader will gain?
- Is it well printed and well set out? Is it easy to read, with plenty of white space and big print? Have you used different type to highlight key points? Does it look interesting?
- Does it contain new information? Is the information presented in an interesting way? Have you checked it for readability and correct spelling? Have you removed all nonessential words?
- Is the information related to the trainees' experiences, knowledge, and vocabulary?
- Are you presenting the information in a succinct, accurate, and logical form?
- Have you broken down large blocks of information into smaller paragraphs with attention-grabbing headings?
- Does it contain simple illustrations and diagrams? Cartoons can be effective and fun.
- Have you given current, relevant examples of each new concept or idea?
- Do you have summaries, questions to be answered, or projects at the end of each section? Is the essential information brought together?
- Have you given references for further reading?
- How are you going to get feedback after the handout has been read?
- How are you going to praise and encourage trainees?

Provide an environment where trainees can learn and enjoy themselves.

8. PLAN EVALUATION

Why Evaluate?

The questions most often asked about any training program are:

a. How effective is it?
b. Is it worth the money?
c. How can the training be improved?

Evaluation of the training course can help provide answers to these questions.

What Is Evaluation?

In simple terms, evaluation can be defined as: "A means of identifying the strengths and weaknesses of a particular activity or program with the aim of making a decision about it."

The decision may be to improve, expand, modify, or cancel it—or even to leave the program unchanged if it is thought to be effective as it stands.

What Are the Main Types of Evaluation?

There are four main types of evaluation:

1. *Reaction evaluation*—measures the reaction of the trainees themselves to the training program or any of its components.

2. *Learning evaluation*—measures change in the trainee's knowledge, attitudes, and practices. A pretraining test (pretest) is compared with posttraining test (posttest) results.

3. *Performance evaluation*—measures how the trainee's job performance has altered after a period of time as a result of training. Performance before training is compared with that after training.

4. *Impact evaluation*—measures the effectiveness of the training by assessing the type and degree of change that the trainees have had on the organization or target group with which they work.

If all these four types of evaluation are carried out effectively, they will show whether the training program is effective or if the money has been well spent. They will also provide information on which areas of the training program should be improved.

In reality, however, it is rarely possible to use all four types of evaluation due to limited resources.

The trainer is responsible for deciding which type of evaluation, if any, will be conducted. The following five examples are given as guidelines for various situations.

Situation 1. If you want *quantitative data* such as the number of courses offered, number of trainees being trained, the duration of training, or the training budget, no formal evaluation needs to be conducted. A *report* with statistics about the training program should be sufficient. It should include:

1. Title and topic of the course.
2. Duration and dates.
3. Number of trainees attending.
4. Total budget used for training.

(A training report should also include information on objectives of the program, activities undertaken, outputs, and evaluation results.)

Situation 2.   If you want to find out whether the trainees are *satisfied with the course* and why, or if the training program needs to be improved and how this could be done, a *reaction evaluation* should be carried out.

To obtain the trainee's reaction to the course, ask general questions such as:

1. What did you like most about the course?
2. What did you dislike most about the course?
3. Did the course achieve its objectives?
4. How could it be improved?

These questions can be asked informally or set out as formal questionnaires for each trainee to complete. The latter is often preferable because the personal reactions of all trainees can be obtained with the minimum influence from their peers. On the other hand, daily informal discussions are very useful because you get immediate feedback.

This information can also be obtained by asking trainees to complete a form such as the one shown in Figure 11. Various aspects of the course are rated on a given scale.

Situation 3.   If you want to find out whether the trainees were able to achieve the *training objectives,* or whether there is any change in their knowledge, attitude, and practices as a result of the training, a *learning evaluation* should be conducted. This should include pre- and posttraining tests.

To test how much the trainees have learned during the course, various tests can be used, including the following:

1. *Essay*—Describe the advantages and limitations of teaching by the lecture method.
2. *Short answer questions*—Answer the following questions: What is learning evaluation? When should it be used? How can it be conducted?
3. *Completion of sentences*—Complete the following: (. . .) evaluation is used to determine the ultimate success of the

FIGURE 11
REACTION EVALUATION FORM
Title and Topic of Course _____ **Date** ___

To help the organizers of the training program improve their course, please rate the training on a scale by drawing a circle around the appropriate number.

	Good	Fair	Poor
	3	2	1
1. Value of this training in relation to my job	3	2	1
2. Presentation method used	3	2	1
3. Training facilities	3	2	1
4. Opportunity for participation	3	2	1
5. Value of handouts	3	2	1
6. Duration of training	3	2	1

training by ascertaining whether the problem has been solved and, if so, if it was due to the training.

4. *True or false questions*—Performance evaluation is used to determine whether the training objectives have been achieved. True/False. (Yes/No answers are also a quick way of finding how much trainees have learned.)

5. *Multiple choice questions*—If you want to teach someone a skill, it is best to:
   a. Show a film of someone doing the job.
   b. Give a lecture on how to do it.
   c. Demonstrate on a model.
   d. Make the trainee do the job with someone supervising each step.

   Please write the correct answer (*a, b, c,* or *d*).

The above are examples of some common forms of tests for knowledge. For attitudes and skills, sample tests are as follows:

1. **Test for attitude**
   Please circle the abbreviation that best fits your opinion.

   Meaning of abbreviations: SA = Strongly agree, A = Agree, D = Disagree, SD = Strongly disagree

   1. Smoking in public buses is reasonable behavior.   SA   A   D   SD
   2. Democracy is the best form of government.   SA   A   D   SD

2. Test for skill

The trainer or an observer fills in a checklist as the trainee performs the required skill. For example: *To test if the trainee can set up an overhead projector.*

Place a check mark (✔) according to what the trainee does.

		Correct	*Wrong*
1.	Make sure there are no distracting light sources.	( )	( )
2.	Find the nearest power source and test to see that it works.	( )	( )
3.	Get a suitable table (height and rigidity are important) and place it in position.	( )	( )
4.	Place overhead projector on table.	( )	( )
5.	Plug in projector making sure the cord is safely out of the way of the audience. (It is a good idea to first wrap the projector cord around the leg of the table. This prevents the projector from crashing to the floor if someone trips on the cord.)	( )	( )
6.	Turn on electric power.	( )	( )
7.	Check that the bulb is working.	( )	( )
8.	Set up the screen, adjusting it to get a 45-degree angle to the projector light beam.	( )	( )
9.	Place a transparency on projector, and focus.	( )	( )
10.	Adjust the table so that the picture fills up the screen.	( )	( )
11.	Move around the room and sit down in various positions to check that the screen can be seen clearly from all parts of the room.	( )	( )

To measure change in a trainee's skill, a test should be given just before the training program and another just after it is completed.

Situation 4.   If you want to study the *job performance* of the trainees after their return to work, carry out a *performance evaluation*. Again, this should include pretests and posttests of the trainees' performance.

To evaluate the performance of trainees after their return to work, use:

a. Observation forms.

b. Questionnaires.

c. Details of work output.

Example.   "After completion of training, the trainee is expected to be able to type in English at a speed of at least 30 words per minute without errors." An observation form to evaluate this performance could be set out as follows:

Name of typist _____

Date _____

1. Typing a given text in English.   No. of mistakes _____

2. Time spent in typing   ____ min ____ secs.

3. Speed of typing   ____words/min.

4. Evaluation   _____

5. Remarks (and possible recommendations)   _____

Another way to assess the typist's performance would be to check the quality of randomly selected work. A speed test should be carried out prior to training as it is only *change* in performance that can be attributed to the training.

Performance evaluations should be given after definite periods of time—say, two weeks, three months, and six months after training.

Situation 5. If you want to find whether the *problems* in an organization or community have been solved when the trainees return to work and whether this is due to the training, carry out an *impact evaluation.* This should include pre- and postassessment of conditions and indicators.

Baseline data should be collected before training starts. Evaluation to determine the impact of training should normally be carried out within the year following training.

This is the most difficult and expensive type of evaluation to carry out. Therefore, it needs to be planned carefully and a budget allocated before the training starts.

Example. *Population education program*

A village in a developing country had a problem of high population growth. One of the older villagers had considerable influence in the village and had expressed concern over the problem. It was proposed that she should receive training in population concepts and family planning. Before this was done, the following data was collected (the baseline indicators):

a. Total population of the community.

b. Total number of births per year.

c. Total number of deaths per year.

d. Number of people leaving the community.

e. Number of people entering the community.

This information allowed calculation of the growth rate of the community before training was carried out [i.e., $(b - c) + (e - d)/a$].

One year after training, the same type of data could be collected again. If there is a decline in the population growth rate, it may be the result of the work of the community leader who has taught family planning methods. It may, however, be nothing to do with the training and could be the result of:

1. Outward migration of people from the village.
2. A sudden increase in the availability of contraceptives.
3. Other factors.

All possible factors should be considered before it can be concluded that the change is the result of training the community leader.

The above situations involve only one type of evaluation (situations 2, 3, 4, and 5) or no formal evaluation (situation 1, which is covered by a report). However, in most cases, decisions are rarely as simple or clear-cut as these, and it may be necessary to conduct more than one type of evaluation.

C. PRESENTATION OF TRAINING ACTIVITIES

FIGURE 12

C. Presentation

9. Conduct training
   - Keep to your lesson plans.
   - Use a variety of methods.
   - Encourage participation.
   - Use demonstrations, models, visual aids.

10. Evaluate training
    - Conduct planned evaluation.
    - Summarize results.
    - Write evaluation report.

11. Review and revise
    - Summarize training.
    - Review in light of the evaluations.
    - Discuss with other trainers involved.
    - Revise to improve relevance.

9. CONDUCT TRAINING

To be a good trainer, you require experience and skill. Experience comes with practice, and skill with evaluations. Here are some helpful hints:

1. Get to know your students—their needs, their ambitions, their humor.
2. The discipline of going back to basics is a valuable learning experience.
3. Little of what we passively listen to is remembered. People learn best by doing things. The more participation you have in your training, the better it will be.
4. The more variety you can get into your training, the more interesting it will be.
5. A good basis for training is "tell—show—ask—discuss—do—review."
6. A good demonstration will save you a lot of talking.
7. Allow plenty of time for trainees to practice new skills.
8. Objective evaluations are important and must be taken notice of. The trainer must be ready to change the content of his course and his training methods—he must be flexible in his attitudes.
9. Use imagination when designing a program.
10. Make your training lively—make it interesting and make it fun.

10. EVALUATE TRAINING

The four main types of evaluation,

a. Reaction evaluation.
b. Learning evaluation.
c. Performance evaluation.
d. Impact evaluation.

are discussed in Section 8 of this chapter at the planning stage. Each should have been considered for evaluation of the effectiveness of the training and the most appropriate type(s) planned and prepared before training began.

When the evaluation is completed, results should be reported for further discussion and action. The most important action to take after a training evaluation is to decide whether to cancel, improve, or modify future training programs.

11. REVIEW AND REVISE

Training should be dynamic. Each group is different, so make your training flexible and relevant to your trainees' needs.

Constantly review, revise, and experiment with your training methods—it's the only way to keep your training fresh, vibrant, and interesting.

The battle cry for this decade will be performance, productivity, and accountability.

Chapter Five

Managing Training

After You Have Read This Chapter, You Should Be Able To:

Prepare Your Own Training Checklists

Organize Residential Courses

Just as the crew of an aircraft has a detailed checklist of instruments to check before take-off, so should trainers before starting training.

A new trainer should prepare his or her own list, then add to or amend it after each course. This makes planning future sessions easier and builds confidence that courses will be a success.

This subject is divided into five suggested checklists:

1. *Before* planning a training course.
2. *Planning* the training.
3. *Preparation* for the course.
4. *Residential course.*
5. *Evaluation.*

Finally, there is a summary table of the main issues to be considered in training activities.

1. BEFORE PLANNING A TRAINING COURSE

How does training fit into the goals of your organization?

Why is training needed?

Who is going to pay?

Who has the authority to approve expenditure, travel, participants' absence from work?

What is the training policy?

Who is to be trained?

How many people are to be trained?

What are their backgrounds? Do they have a job description containing title, function, objectives, acceptable standards of performance, and responsibilities?

What are their needs? Do you need to carry out a job analysis?

What do they need to be taught?

What resources have you?

How much time is available?

How are trainees to be selected?

2. PLANNING THE TRAINING

A. Objectives
Decide on training objectives and write them down.

Be specific and precise.

Describe the desired result.

Describe a change you can measure or observe.

What criteria can you use to judge success?

List conditions where results can be achieved.

How will you know when you have achieved your objectives?

What new tasks will the trainees be able to do?

B. Methods
Where are you going to carry out training?

What sort of training are you going to carry out—job-related training, training to overcome a problem, or teaching new techniques or new skills?

What topics are to be covered?
Both top management and participants should be involved in deciding on the course content, and both should be consulted during the course.

How are you going to teach topics?
Aim to get as much participation as possible.

Design the course and break it up into learning experiences.

3. PREPARATION FOR THE COURSE

Decide on the training methods you will use.

Select instructors, contact them to see if they are available, and brief them on what is required.

What training aids are needed? Check the rooms to see if electricity is available, if you can darken the room for films, etc. Check on availability of training aids such as blackboards, paper pads, overhead projectors, film projectors, white boards, etc.

Are the rooms suitable for training?

Are they quiet?

Can the trainer be heard easily in all parts of the room?

Is lighting adequate?

Can rooms be adequately ventilated and air-conditioned or heated if necessary?

What seating arrangement is to be used—circular, U-shaped, or square?

Do you need tables for writing?

Recheck that all necessary equipment will be available when required and in good working order.

Prepare lesson plans but be flexible, allowing time for extra discussions or more practical work.

Prepare handouts.

Are you going to print proceedings of the course? If so, contact reporters, typist, editors, printers, etc.

4. RESIDENTIAL COURSE

Prepare a budget.

Book accommodation for participants and any visiting instructors.

Make travel arrangements.

Organize meals and coffee breaks.

Prepare information for support staff, instructors, management, and servicing people such as caterers, cooks, audiovisual technicians, librarians, caretakers, and drivers. All necessary instructions and details of number of trainees, times of arrival, etc., should be given in writing.

Prepare printed information for trainees. This should include:
  A message welcoming course members.
  Outline of objectives (what is expected from trainees).
  Detailed timetable. Make sure you allow adequate time for
    participants to get from place to place.
  Statement on costs; also, information on any sponsorships or
    subsidies that might be available.

List of course members and where they come from.
Map of area showing meeting rooms, office, sleeping
     accommodations, toilet facilities, bus stops, shops, etc.
Note of any relevant training area regulations.
Advice on possible health problems. Where to go, whom to see,
     likely costs, and payment procedures.
Names and whereabouts of persons who are available when
     help is needed.
Note on room-cleaning arrangements, laundry facilities (where
     and when available), and bed-linen changes.
Library hours and rules.
Note on recreation facilities—types and times available, rules,
     and any charges to be paid.
Advice on locking rooms and putting valuables into
     safekeeping.
Location of nearest shopping facilities (availability of writing
     materials, toilet gear, stamps, snacks, etc.)
Correct postal address for trainees. Where to collect and post
     mail, local postal charges.
Mealtimes, times for morning and afternoon breaks.
Person to contact for any special diet requirements.
Public transport services—where to get buses/trains, their
     frequency and cost.
Location of various churches, temples, or mosques,
     approximate distances from training center, and times of
     prayers and services.
Nearest banking facilities.
Name and location of person with overall responsibility for
     organizing and administering course. Times when he/she is
     available.
Advice on how return-travel arrangements are to be confirmed.
Trainees will also appreciate tourist-type publicity brochures
     and a map of the local area.

5. EVALUATION

How will you know if training has been successful?

How effective has it been?

Was it worth the money expended?

How could a similar course be improved?

How will you evaluate? How often? Which of the following four
methods will you use?

1. Reaction evaluation.
2. Learning evaluation.
3. Performance evaluation.
4. Impact evaluation. See Chapter 4 for examples.

FIGURE 13
Training Checklist

	Specific Answers Required, Persons to Be Contacted, etc.	Date to Be Completed	Done ✔
1. Who approves training? manages training?			
2. Who are the trainees? Trainers? Support staff?			
3. Why is there a need for training? What is the training policy?			
4. How much money is available? What is the length of the course?			
5. What are the course objectives? What subjects are to be taught? What jobs are to be done? Who will do them?			
6. When should planning be done? When should preparation be done? When is the presentation? When will the evaluation be done?			
7. Where will the training be carried out? Which rooms? laboratory? workshop? fields? others?			
8. Who will do what? when? where? why? how?			

FIGURE 13 (*Concluded*)

	Specific Answers Required, Persons to Be Contacted, etc.	Date to Be Completed	Done ✔
9. What materials are needed? List equipment, supplies, audiovisuals, handouts, etc.			
10. Have all trainees been given clear, written instructions about the course?			
11. Have you double-checked arrangements for accomodation? catering? travel?			
12. Have you evaluated the course?			
13. Have you written a report and completed the budget?			
14. Have you written to thank instructors, hostel managers, etc.?			

Chapter Six

Participative Training

After You Have Read This Chapter, You Should Be Able To:

Set Up Working Groups

Introduce Participative Training into Your Courses

Participative training is a "learning through sharing and doing" activity. It is often called "discovery," "experiential," or "action" learning.

Participants are involved in activities designed to share experiences and discover new information. It can be used with groups of varying sizes.

Basically, it is discovering one's needs and sharing knowledge about satisfying them, while developing interpersonal skills.

Participative training can be a very effective training method because we are more likely to remember a solution we have worked out for ourselves than one thought out for us. Also, we are more likely to act on decisions we have made for ourselves.

Some Examples of Participative Training

Discussion groups.

Competitive groups.

Role-playing groups.

Simulation exercises.

Workshops.

Seminars.

Forums.

Tutorials.

Contests.

Quizzes.

Debates.

ENVIRONMENT

Arrange the room for interaction.

Round tables take the emphasis off the trainer and help promote participation.

Tables set up to form a square, or chairs set in a circle, establish equality between participants and trainer and help promote group discussion.

U shapes, too, promote interaction but establish the trainer as authority.

THE THREE BASICS

There are three basic requirements for successful instruction.

1. *Involvement.* Involve your trainees as much as possible.
2. *Accountability.* Trainees must realize they are responsible for their own learning.
3. *Feedback.* Tell trainees how they are progressing but also evaluate your own training methods to see which ones are the most successful.

GETTING STARTED

- Allow time for trainees and tutors to get acquainted. This helps build a climate of trust and makes it easier for learners to relax and respond.
- Start by dividing the class into pairs. Get them talking on a comfortable topic, such as "My hobbies and interests outside work" or "My job." Ask each person to report on what they learned about their partner.
- Get learners involved as soon as possible. Make them feel they can contribute. Let them share their experiences and ideas. This also gives the trainer a chance to appraise the group.
- Introduce games, role-playing, and competitions early. It helps energize the group and build group cohesion.
- Chaining is a good warm-up technique. In *chaining,* the trainer aims to get a series of responses, each of which leads to the next. A topical, controversial subject is best (e.g., "Trade is more important than aid"). Get each person to stand and speak

for one minute. The next person must continue in logical sequence without repeating previous arguments.

- Set training goals early in the course. Start off with pairs on a topic such as "My training goals" or "What I hope to get out of this training." Each person then stands and reports to the full group. This leads to an analysis of the training objectives.

- After pairing exercises, form groups of three (triads). Get the group to discuss questions that are controversial (e.g., "How can we improve our office communications?" or "What is the biggest work problem we have?"). You can ask one person to act as the chairperson and report group findings to the full meeting.

- Allow thinking time. When you set a problem, don't be in a hurry to start. Allow trainees to make a few notes first or have a general discussion before you start group exercises. Perhaps you could send them off in pairs for a walk to discuss the subject and "warm up" so they are ready to record their ideas for reporting back to the full meeting.

When you involve learners you improve retention.

DIVIDE INTO WORKING GROUPS

1. The Traditional Way

After counting the number of participants, decide on the number of groups and the size of each group. For example, if there are 21 participants and you want three groups, you can count off groups of seven or number them off, "One, two, three. One, two, three, etc. All the 'Ones' here, the 'Twos' there, and the 'Threes' in this corner." Then send groups off to elect their own leaders.

2. The Democratic Way

Hand out a sheet of paper. Ask participants to write down the name of one person they would like as a leader. Collect them and count to see who are the most popular choices. The winners of the ballot come forward and draw lots to see who selects first. (Break off three match sticks at different lengths and let each leader have a draw. The person with the longest has first choice, and so on.)

They take turns at selecting participants for their group.

Write the names in each group on a blackboard or use an overhead projector so all can see.

3. The Autocratic Way

Prior to the activity, the trainer selects the participants to make up balanced groups. Lists are printed and handed out.

Guidelines

After the groups have been established, set up training guidelines. Make the rules as democratic as possible. For example:

- There will be no rank in the training room—all are equal.
- Say what you honestly think.
- Only one person to speak at a time.
- Make a special effort to listen carefully to all discussions.
- Be brief with your comments.
- Anything said in groups is confidential. Only group conclusions will be reported to the whole meeting.
- Be punctual and try to attend every session.

Use of Participative Methods

- To identify, explore, and seek solutions to problems.
- To develop plans for action.
- Where necessary, to change attitudes through an amicable examination of the evidence.
- To develop leadership skills.
- As a supplementary technique in many types of training.

Advantages

- Groups pool experiences, abilities, and knowledge to reach recognized goals.
- Allows every member to participate fully.
- Can establish a democratic consensus.
- Can stimulate a desire to learn and to share.
- Often one individual's enthusiasm can stimulate the whole group.

Limitations

- Can be time consuming, particularly if persons with strong convictions or widely different backgrounds are involved.
- Preliminary exercises are needed before serious group activity is possible.

Requirements

- A skilled chairperson (or leader) is needed to prevent the more dominant members from taking over the group.
- Participants should sit in a circle or rectangle in an informal, relaxed atmosphere that is free from noise and other distractions.
- "Face-to-face" discussion is essential.
- Discussion is usually less restrained when a group is small. The effectiveness of group discussion may decline when there are more than 7 people in a group or when there are more than 30 in the workshop. (A workshop of 28, for example, could be appropriately divided into four groups of 7, and if these were balanced in terms of age, personality, and experience, conditions would be ideal for training.)
- Each group should appoint a chairperson (or leader) and a reporter.

Preparation and Procedure

- Be sure your instructions to groups are clear, precise, and, preferably, written (for easy reference). For example:

    "Topic . . . .
    It is now 2 P.M.
    You have 1 hour in which to

    - Appoint a reporter.
    - Discuss the topic and bring down recommendations to solve the problems.

    It is suggested that you

    - Break the topic into workable "bites."
    - Arrange your recommendations in their order of priority.
    - Appoint a spokesperson to report your findings to the full meeting.

- Arrange for your reporter to hand the tutor a copy of your findings.

Report back at 3 P.M."

- Start off with exercises that are interesting, topical, and appropriate for the group.

Hints

- Group cooperation should be stressed at an early stage. A good approach is to introduce a controversial topic for discussion but without any guidelines. Such a discussion inevitably grows heated: it is not always relevant; there is disagreement on procedures; personality clashes occur; and one or two people monopolize all the available time.
  Ask the group to discuss what happened without a chairperson and rules. Having experienced the difficulties of unguided discussion, most people will be interested in learning the mechanics of group interaction, and later discussions will be more productive.

Observation exercise. A helpful exercise is to split a large group into two working parties, one of which discusses a controversial topic while the other sits *silently* and observes. Brief the groups separately, keeping the briefing simple. For example, the observers could be told:

- "Each of you is to sit behind a member of the working group, but not close enough to cause distraction."
- "Draw a simple diagram to record the discussion pattern."

Encourage the observers to identify various types of behavior. They should be able to identify which member

Asks the most questions.

Provides the best information.

Acts as guide.

Talks about the group.

Seeks and encourages ideas.

Settles the arguments.

Is content just to follow.

Keeps the group happy.

FIGURE 14

The lines in this example show that A spoke to B three times, C asked four questions of D, and so on. This provides a general picture of the group's most active members.

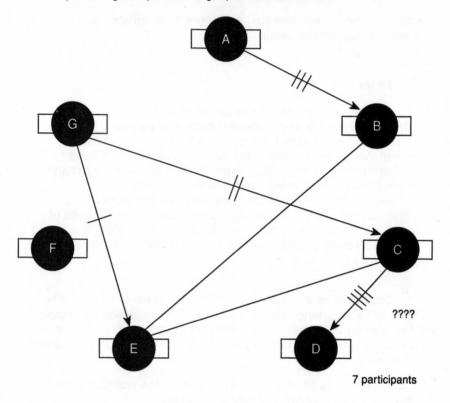

7 participants

Imposes his opinion on the rest.

Does not contribute at all.

Ask for comments on any other interesting behavior. For example:

"Have you noticed any changes in the relationship between various members?"

"Has the group's attitude as a whole changed?"

"Has an obvious leader emerged?"

"Did any real plan evolve?"

The main points to observe here are the progress of the group as a whole and the interaction of its members.

At the end of the observation exercise, ask the groups to reverse their roles (i.e., the observation group now becomes the discussion group).

Give the new discussion group a topic that is relevant to group discussion. For example: "What conclusions can be drawn about the effectiveness of group discussion?" or "How can the workings of a discussion group be improved?" or "What are the advantages and disadvantages of formality in groups?"

At the conclusion of this exercise, bring the groups together for a general discussion. Draw up some practical guidelines that can be applied to future sessions, such as:

- One member should not be allowed to dominate.

- Any shy members must be encouraged.

- Private conversations hinder group discussion and should be discouraged.

Observations on Group Dynamics

- The size of the group is important. Small groups encourage more active participation.

- A group's effectiveness depends on the personalities of its members.

- Its effectiveness also depends on the style of leadership.

- Social pressures in a group can be very strong and, if not closely watched, can hinder progress.

- Any adverse criticism must relate to an *idea* and not to its originator. (Personal criticism can lead to the "injured" member withdrawing from any further discussion.)

- A video replay can provide a useful analysis of group dynamics. When participants become accustomed to having a camera in the room, they will start to act naturally. Two "operators" will be needed—one to operate the camera and the other to maintain an accurate time sequence, so that any particular section can be found easily in a replay. The filming should concentrate on wide-angle shots of the whole group, but the occasional close-up will highlight a point and identify the "doodlers," the "chatterers," or the "dozers."

  Participative training is a powerful training tool. It is learning through sharing and doing. But don't forget that when you are talking you will not be learning.

In teaching there should be no class distinctions.

                                                                Confucius

Chapter Seven

Training Ways

After You Have Read This Chapter, You Should Be Able To:

Identify a Wider Range of Training Methods

Select More Effective Training Ways for Your Courses and Workshops

Establish a Rapport with Your Trainees

WHICH METHOD?

There are many different ways to teach. Too many tutors have too few tools in their teaching kits.

A particular group was asked to list and then to classify all the teaching methods they could think of. Figure 15 shows the list they made. Do you agree with it and with their classifications? Can you think of any methods they have left out? Are any of them wrongly classified?

VARIETY IS IMPORTANT

Be sure your program is flexible. Build flexibility into the training. Provide some uncertainty, some variety, some competition, and some entertainment. We learn best when we enjoy our learning and are spurred into competing. It has been said that "Variety is the spice of life." The same is true for training.

MENTAL PEAKS

The good teacher exploits the naturally occurring concentration peaks. For most of us, our concentration intensifies in the late morning. It drops off sharply straight after lunch, but there is normally another peak after the afternoon break.

FIGURE 15
Teaching Aids

Active	Inactive
Spoken Seminar, group discussion, evaluating, question period, conversing, simulation exercise, interview	Lecture, visit, observation session, forum, telephone calls, song, role-playing, conference, debating, panel discussions, radio program, talk, questions, suggestion, slogans, poetry, demonstrations, coaching, home visiting, taped programs, workshop, tutorials
Written Assignment, directed reading, survey, games, projects, crossword puzzles, "filling-in" forms, problem solving	Letters, brochures, bulletins, manuals, circulars, leaflets, case studies, newsletters, reports, regulations, books, magazines, newspapers, "filling-in" blanks
Visual Constructing visual aids, models, amassing a collection, actual object, display	Sighting real objects, slides, diagrams, cartoon, blackboard, graphs, chart, transparencies, overhead projectors, models, displays, photographs, poster, wall newspapers, maps, puppet show, exhibitions, trade fairs, field tours, drama, epidiascope, drawings, flannelgraph, display board, magnetic board, albums, histogram, samples, observations, advertisements, symbols, picture story
Audiovisual Videotape recorders	Demonstration, tape-slide shows, filmstrips (with commentaries), display, films, cartoon, field day, "tours," closed-circuit television

Organize the teaching program around these peaks. Introduce new material or a difficult concept when mental activity is running high. Naturally there is some individual variation, but most people cannot concentrate hard for more than about 20 minutes at a time. If you must have lengthy sessions, break off periodically for a rest and, perhaps, a walk.

Arrange for periods of shared activity while mental activity is low. The experienced tutor often allows an extended lunchtime break during a difficult program or arranges a group discussion in which everybody is involved soon after the lunch break.

You can help people to keep alert by introducing an element of novelty into your program—"I am going to spin this pen. When it stops, the person it points to will be asked to lead the next session."

EXPERIMENTING

The experienced tutor will also experiment with different training techniques. When a plumber goes out on a job, he takes a kit full of different tools. You, too, should examine the job you will be undertaking and then select the most appropriate tools from your bagful of teaching techniques. When you have assessed a particular group, choose one of the "tried and tested" teaching methods. If it is successful, build from there—if it fails, pick out a different method and try again.

KNOWLEDGE, SKILLS, AND ATTITUDES

The trainer will generally break down the course objectives into three main categories—knowledge, skills, and attitudes.

Knowledge can be transmitted in a lecture by using visual aids and handouts, but the development of a *skill* requires repeated practice. Start from the stage your course members have reached, and build their skills and confidence gradually. Don't try to teach too much at one time. Behavioral skills take time to develop. With a lifetime's accumulation of *attitudes* in each of us, we cannot expect to change them very rapidly.

SELECTING THE BEST METHOD

Have a Clear Objective

What action do you want your course members to take after their course is finished? How will you know whether you have been successful?

Time Required

Most trainers are too ambitious and they achieve very little. Allow plenty of time for adequate discussion and thinking.

Choosing Your Environment

If, for example, you intend to break the course into small groups, don't handicap them with a formal lecture hall as the setting.

Doing Your Homework

It is important for you to learn as much as you can about your students beforehand. If this proves too difficult, build in some early exercises that will help you to assess. For example, you might divide the group into pairs and ask the members of each pair to talk to one another about their hobbies and family and work experiences. Then ask each one in turn to report to the full group on what they have found out about their partner. (See Chapter 4, Section A, "Planning.")

Proven Exercises First

Start with the exercises you feel confident will work. (Don't forget, however, to introduce new ways of teaching from time to time, in order to build up your kit of teaching tools.) If, after experimenting, you find you have a failure on your hands, talk it out with the members themselves as a group learning experience. Never apologize for a failure, but do make sure you profit from the experience.

Before You Start Choosing

As a first step, the course should be broken down into a series of units or subjects. When you and the course members have agreed on a clear objective, it is a good idea to set them to work in small groups, on suggesting the topics they believe should be covered. The secret of success is to involve every member and to call on their experience.

Which Methods?

Having defined your subject area, your objectives, and the course contents, you should review the various teaching methods that are available and could be used. For example, a supervision or management course could include:

Lectures.

Case studies.

Problem-solving exercises.

Work exercises.

Book and journal reviews.

Small-group discussions.

Group competitions.

Role-playing ("simulation exercises").

Introducing guests.

Experience at chairing.

Votes of thanks.

Initiative exercises.

Generating ideas (brainstorming), etc.

Choose Carefully

Whichever exercises you select, make sure they are related to the members' "back home" situation. Never "import" someone else's exercises, out of a "foreign" book. Your students must see their training as relevant to their lives and important to their jobs.

Plan for Some Carryover

Whenever possible, you should help each member to draw up a detailed plan for personal action, to ensure the new behavior patterns learned during the course will be put into practice back on the job.

But beware of starting a revolution. Quiet evolution is usually more acceptable and often achieves faster results. If their old social ties are resisting their new behavior pattern, the whole course could prove to be just a waste of time and the members will be frustrated. In a formal organization, acceptance of the course and full support of it by the top management are vital prerequisites. Get full support from top management before you start training.

Establish Your Credentials

Your first job must be to establish a rapport with your audience. Start with the exercises you like and with which you feel confident. Don't be in a hurry. Take your time, chat away, tell a few stories about yourself, and make sure that every member of the course becomes fully involved as soon as possible.

The devices you use will depend on

Your experience.

Your audience.

Your environment.

Your subject.

The time you have available.

Your objectives.

Don't Talk too Much

Trainers tend to talk too much. Learn to focus on key issues and lead with questions.

There is nothing wrong with change if it's in the right direction.

Sir Winston Churchill

Chapter Eight

Training Techniques

After You Have Read This Chapter, You Should Be Able To:

Know the Advantages and Disadvantages of a Wide Range of Training Techniques

Add Variety to Your Training by Using Different Methods

Solve Problems Using a Five-step Method

Many trainers and tutors spend too much time giving lectures that their students find irrelevant and boring. Participative training is usually more interesting, enjoyable, and effective. It is always more challenging.

Add variety to your training by using some of the techniques listed below. The training methods are explained; their uses, advantages, and limitations are discussed; and hints are given for new trainers. They are listed in alphabetical order for ease of reference.

Audience-reaction team

Brainstorming (see Generating ideas)

"Buzz" session

Case study

Committee

Computer-based training

Conference

Convention

Debate

Demonstration

Discussion group

Drama spots (see Role-playing)

Exercise

Exhibit

Film

Forum

Games and simulations

Generating ideas (Brainstorming)

Interview

Lecture

Listening team

Multimedia package

Panel

Peer teaching (Peer-assisted learning, Peer-mediated instruction)

Programmed instruction

Question time

Role-playing and drama spots

Seminar

Short course

Simulations (see Games)

Skit

Speech (see Lecture)

Symposium

Teleconference (An electronic get-together)

Video

Visit, field trip, or tour

Workshop

AUDIENCE-REACTION TEAM

A representative sample of three to five audience members is on stage with the speaker in order to clarify points that might not otherwise be understood. They ask questions of the speaker (or some resource person) either during or at the end of an address. A useful technique when an audience is very large or whenever it would be difficult to accept questions from the floor.

Uses

• Facilitates communication on a difficult subject.

- Provides audience feedback, enabling the speaker to gain a sample view of a large audience.
- Can lead a discussion at the end of an address and thus "draw out" the speaker.

Advantages

- Easy to organize (but make sure the speaker is experienced enough to cope with such a team).
- Helps the expert who is not a good communicator to get the message across.
- Its presence may stimulate audience interest.

Limitations

- The speaker may object to a supposed inference that he/she is a poor communicator (or to being interrupted during the presentation).
- The audience's role is passive.
- Some team members may "overparticipate" (show off), while others may be too timid for the job.
- Sometimes upsets a speaker.

Requirements

- Raised platform or stage, large enough for a speaker's rostrum, the chairman, and the team members.
- Every member of the audience should be able to see and hear each speaker.

Preparation and Procedure

- Organizer must discuss the technique fully with the guest speaker and gain approval to proceed.
- Chairman, guest speaker, and team meet together.
- Chairman introduces the topic to the full audience and describes the technique and the rules (also team's function and the reasons for using it).

- Chairman introduces the speaker (brief remarks on position held, experience, and any relevant special qualifications).
- Team reacts at the agreed-upon times.

Hints

- Select team members very carefully.
- Beware—unless your speaker is enthusiastic and confident, the team may cause undesirable tension.

"BUZZ" SESSION

A technique to involve a large audience directly in the discussion process by dividing up the members into small groups of five, six, or seven for a limited time (5 to 15 minutes) to discuss a specific topic, with each member contributing to the discussion.

Uses

- To decide on questions for a speaker or panel.
- To decide on adequacy of available information.
- To plan future events.
- To produce recommendations.
- To evaluate a meeting or event.

Advantages

- Gives everyone a chance to participate without embarrassment.
- Gets people involved.
- Can become a source of fresh ideas.
- Competitive groups can provide a stimulating experience.

Limitations

- Individual participation is limited by time.
- Group contributions may be contradictory or difficult to reconcile.

- A skilled organizer is required.
- Difficult with large groups.

Requirements

- Chairs that are easy to rearrange.
- If numbers permit, use open-formation seating (a circle or a U arrangement is ideal because no one is hidden); avoid theater-type seating.
- Cards or papers for note taking (most people carry a pen).

Preparation and Procedure

- Calculate approximate number in audience.
- Work out the number of groups you will have (for example, an audience of 28 could provide four groups of 7).
- Having decided on four groups, you would quickly number off the audience from one to four.
- Gather all the number ones in one part of the room, the twos in another part, and so on. ("Right. All the ones here please.")
- Each group is instructed to select a leader and a recorder.
- The leader's job is to see that everyone has a chance to speak.
- The recorder summarizes the discussion.
- At the end of the session, the leader or the recorder of each group reports orally to the full meeting.
- The organizer and an assistant collect and summarize all the reports and process them.

Hints

- Time is saved by the organizer nominating the leaders and the recorders.
- A good technique to gather additional information for a resource speaker and for setting up questions.
- Set up the groups before the lecture and ask each one to carry out "selective listening." For example:
  - Group 1—notes points that require further amplification.
  - Group 2—looks for omissions on which you would like the speaker's view.

- Group 3—lists points with which you disagree.
- Can be used to get more out of a technical film by providing it with greater purpose.

CASE STUDY

Comprehensive oral, written, and/or filmed account of an event or series of related events.

Uses

- Presents a situation problem for discussion.
- Problem-solving technique.
- Teaching problem-solving processes.
- Builds up a complete picture.

Advantages

- Provides relevant detail.
- Helps to identify alternative solutions.
- Helps to develop analytical, problem-solving skills.

Limitations

- Can be time consuming.
- Relevance may not always be obvious.
- Stimulates some people but irritates others.

Requirements

They will vary with the type of case—a stage or some other, fully visible area will be needed if you are going to act out a problem; a film calls for a blackout and for a suitable screen and projector (check on their availability well beforehand).

Procedure

- Chairman introduces the topic and explains the case study and what is required.

- Chairman guides the discussion toward achieving the desired result.

Hints

- Allow plenty of time before the start for members to study a written case.
- Can be very effective if small groups compete in seeking solutions.
- A debate on possible solutions can be worthwhile when a capable chairman is available to keep the speakers on course.
- Some red herrings are desirable in any case study, but take care not to build in too many at the expense of getting the main message across.
- Don't waste time in looking for a scapegoat.
- The best case studies are built upon actual problems (but take care to hide the identity of the people involved).
- A common technique in management courses is to ask each member to describe an office problem as a case study for group solution, and later reveal (and sometimes discuss) how it was in fact handled.

COMMITTEE

Small group selected to act on behalf of the entire group or organization. May function as an executive committee or house committee, and may be further broken down into subcommittees or task forces.

Uses

- Represents an organization between its annual meetings.
- To plan, promote, and organize a special event, such as a seminar or convention.
- As an advisory group.
- To study a particular problem and to bring down recommendations for solving it.
- Evaluating a particular occasion.

Advantages

- Makes use of people with experience and the time to carry out special assignments.
- Utilizes a variety of different interests and experiences.
- Provides a good training ground for future leaders.

Limitations

- Difficulty of appointing a compatible team.
- Often difficult to find enough people with the time and capability to assume the responsibility.
- Must act on behalf of whole organization and needs its support, which sometimes is not given.

Requirements

- An environment that will promote communication.
- Facilities for reaching and recording decisions.

Procedure

- Normally democratically elected by whole organization, but can be appointed by the president or other elected officers (especially applies to subcommittees, working parties, or task forces).
- Should be given a set of rules or guidelines (in large organizations they form a constitution).
- Often required to carry out a particular assignment and to report back to the whole organization or its representatives.
- Such a committee is then given further instructions or is dissolved.

Hints

- A committee's instructions should always be clear—what is expected and when.
- A committee usually needs a chairman to lead it and a secretary to record its findings, decisions, and

recommendations, and to organize the venue and time of its meetings.

- A committee that is faced with a formidable task can be broken up into subcommittees in which selected members are given areas of responsibility and the power to co-opt their own working parties.
- Committee work should enable the less experienced person to work alongside and to profit from the expertise of the more experienced.

COMPUTER-BASED TRAINING (CBT)

Training using a computer to perform rapid calculations and compile, correlate, and select data to support and enhance skill development.

Uses

- Ideal for distance learning, especially for companies with a dispersed work force.
- To standardize training and feedback.
- Good for practicing a skill until proficient.
- Can design a course to the capability of each learner.

Advantages

- Can reduce the cost of training.
- Can reduce time off work and expenses if trainees have to travel for a training program.
- Can save on training accommodation costs.
- Can increase the effectiveness of training.
- Can reduce the length of training.
- Can be used to give more timely training.
- Training can be at any time, day or night.
- Can reduce the amount of equipment needed for training and the damage done to equipment (e.g., airplane flight stimulator).
- Often a better student-to-instructor ratio than other methods.

Limitations

- Expensive to develop. Small companies can rarely afford the costs. Purchased packages are often not suited to the trainees' needs.
- Takes a longer time to develop and test than conventional training courses.
- Trainees need to be computer literate.

Requirements

- A quiet place to study.
- A computer with appropriate learning disks. For distant learning, a modem connected to an additional telephone line.
- Experience in using a computer.

Procedure

- Read the written instructions.
- Load the disk or call up the program using the modem.
- Read the computer instructions and skip through the program.
- Work through the first module. Keep repeating until you have mastered the skills.
- Move on to the next module.
- Discuss your difficulties and experiences with your tutor or a group of other learners.

Hints

- Before you start, upgrade your keyboard and computer skills, if necessary.
- Become familiar with your keyboard.
- Set a specific time aside on a regular basis for study and keep to the routine.
- Choose a quiet time when you are mentally active—not after a heavy meal!
- Computer-based training works best when used with other

training methods. Learners should come together in groups for discussions and guidance from a tutor from time to time.

A personal computer without a telephone line attached to it is a poor lonely thing.

CONFERENCE

Large or small group of people with common interests meeting together by common consent.

Uses

- A group with a common interest discusses a narrow technical area (Conference on Depletion of Ozone in the Atmosphere).
- To develop promotion plans (Conference on Advertising Our National Parks).

Advantages

- Members usually discuss topics of high interest to them.
- Members are usually voluntary attenders.
- Enthusiasts are brought together to share their expertise and to plan.

Limitations

- Often hard to predict number who will attend.
- Arrangements must often be made to provide for guest speakers, a venue, catering, accommodation, and various other costs for an unknown number.
- Degree of success is often hard to measure.

Requirements

- Auditorium, comfortable seating, small meeting rooms, catering facilities, toilets, transport arrangements, accommodation, special equipment for the media and for speakers, audiovisual aids, display facilities, notice boards, etc.

- Promotion and prepublicity, registrations, compiling and publishing program, handouts, and post-publicity.
- Accurate evaluating and follow-up procedures.

Hints

- People need to be told "What's in it for me?"—a clear objective is needed.
- Decide on those you wish to invite. Find out their background and the extent of their information.
- Early program planning is desirable. (The best way to finalize speakers is to visit them or tell them by telephone what the conference is all about, what is expected from them, and who will be attending.) Details should then be sent to the speakers.
- A wide range of publicity is desirable.
- Look after your guest speakers as well—delegate someone to look after and to fuss over each one of them, and don't forget a follow-up thank-you letter.
- Post-conference publicity is just as important as prepublicity— try to get messages to the people who were unable to attend.
- Balance the books and pay the bills as soon after the conference as possible.

CONVENTION

An assembly of representatives of the regional groups of a parent organization.

Uses

- Educational (guest speakers, forums, workshops, and so on).
- To plan policies, objectives, and strengthening strategies.
- To elect officers or candidates.
- As a training ground.
- For any combination of these uses.

Advantages

- An educational experience for individuals from a wide geographic area.

- Can produce a consensus from the many local groups that may make up an organization.
- Provides the individual with a chance to get to know the organization and to see it in action.
- Helps to share experiences and to make contacts.
- Helps to guide and train new appointees to local positions.

Limitations

- Considerable work on advance planning and promotion is required.
- Can be costly.
- Needs an environment that is ideal for large numbers.
- The individual can be made to feel insignificant.
- A group whose ideas or remits are rejected may be resentful.

Requirements

- For the general sessions, a large auditorium in which everybody can see and hear in comfort.
- A number of small meeting rooms.
- Support services—production and audiovisual.
- Adequate sleeping accommodations.
- Catering facilities, toilets, etc.
- Transport.

Preparation and Procedure

- Plan on a national scale.
- Set up sufficient local working parties.
- Carefully plan arrangements for adequate facilities.
- Draw up and publish program details advising key members as soon as possible.
- Advertise.
- Appoint and brief the chairman.
- Opening session with a keynote address.

- Summary, educational, and business sessions.
- Cocktail sessions and/or a formal dinner.
- Final summary sessions (reviewing and so on).
- Such evaluating and follow-up as is needed.

Hints

- The organizer is to coordinate the planning and see that it is implemented on time (check and double-check this)—not to do the actual work.
- Local working parties must be involved at an early stage in the planning.
- The organizer should delegate areas of responsibility to reliable people, who should be given the power to co-opt their own working parties.
- Good communications are necessary from the start of the planning.
- Guest speakers and "draw cards" need to be signed up and briefed early.

DEBATE

A formal contest in which participants present opposing views on a controversial topic. This can take the form of an argument between two people, but in most formal debates there are two teams, each with three members. (A formal debate is a good participative training method involving many people as debators, chairperson, time-keeper, judges, and often commentators from the audience.)

Uses

- To examine a subject in depth and work out arguments for and against a given point of view.
- To show how essential it is to research a subject thoroughly.
- To make participants think logically.
- To help participants think and speak concisely.
- To develop team spirit among the participants.

Advantages

- An active learning experience involving many people.
- Often more interesting than a lecture.
- Useful in changing attitudes.
- Teaches participants to think rapidly in front of an audience and to cope with interjections.

Limitations

- Time consuming. A great deal of research and preparation must be done before the debate if it is to be successful.
- Must be run as a formal event with chairperson, judges, and audience.
- Some participants may be too self-conscious or timid to debate successfully.

Requirements

- Six people (i.e., two teams of three members) who are enthusiastic and prepared to speak on a given topic.
- An interesting, controversial subject with wide audience appeal. The topic should be stated clearly and affirmatively (e.g., "That A should be B," *not* "That A should not be B.") The affirmative team must then debate that the statement is correct, while the negative team must deny or contradict, trying to prove that the statement is false.
- Access to a library for research on the topic.
- A skilled chairperson or moderator.
- Competent judges.
- An audience.
- A set of rules familiar to both teams.
- A timekeeper with stopwatch, bell, or warning lights.
- A suitable venue, preferably with a stage or raised platform with seating for seven people.

Preparation and Procedure

- The chairperson or moderator has complete control of the meeting and sits between the teams. The affirmative team sits at the chairperson's right.

- The chairperson reads the rules of debate to the teams and audience.
- The chairperson is responsible for the times allowed for speakers but may appoint a timekeeper.
- The usual time allowed is 10 minutes for the leaders' opening speeches and 8 minutes for all subsequent speeches.
- Order of debate

  1. Leader of affirmative team.
  2. Leader of negative team.
  3. Second speaker—affirmative.
  4. Second speaker—negative.
  5. Third speaker—affirmative.
  6. Third speaker—negative.
  7. Concluding address by leader of negative team, summarizing their arguments. No fresh material should be introduced at this stage.
  8. Closing address by leader of affirmative team.

- Speakers should address the chairperson but face the audience.
- The leaders should define the subject clearly and concisely.
- The timekeeper should give a warning one minute before the allocated time and again at the final time. Speakers are usually penalized if they exceed their times.
- Speakers who believe they have been misrepresented, or a leader who believes new arguments are being introduced in an opponent's concluding address, may rise to a point of order. The chairperson must give a ruling immediately.
- The timekeeper can extend a speaker's time to compensate for the time taken up by a point of order.
- Members of the opposing team can interject during a speech if the interjections are concise and relevant.
- Judges usually allocate points or marks for:

  Definition of the subject.
  Subject matter.
  Eloquence.
  Deportment.
  Criticism.
  Summary and Conclusion.

- If teams score equal marks, the team whose leader scores the most points in the closing address is judged the winner.

Hints

- Make training fun by selecting humorous topics and witty speakers.
- Select topics carefully. A good topic should give both teams an equal chance of winning.
- Speakers should be advised to:

    1. Clarify the subject.
    2. State arguments clearly. Back them up with evidence and illustrate them with anecdotes.
    3. Restate the arguments briefly.

- Don't waste time while the judges are totaling their marks and preparing comments on performances. Encourage audience participation by asking them for comments or getting them to indicate which team they thought was the winner by a show of hands.

DEMONSTRATION

The performance of an action (or the explanation of a procedure) before an audience to enable the viewers to perform the same action (under guidance, if necessary).

Uses

- To teach a particular task.
- To introduce a new procedure or technique.
- To reinforce a point.
- To introduce a new product.
- To illustrate or dramatize some point in a training program.

Advantages

- What is seen is more likely to be believed and remembered than what is heard or read.

- Trying to do something is a good way to learn.
- The pace can be flexible and the action can be repeated as often as necessary.
- Can use the real thing or a model of it.

Limitations

- More suitable for small groups.
- Can be expensive and time consuming.
- Can cause transport and setting-up problems.
- Special conditions (such as a raised platform) are often required.

Requirements

- The provision of adequate facilities is most important. Everybody must be able to see and to practice with the demonstration equipment. Power points, good lighting, and a raised platform may be other essentials. For a large-scale demonstration, a barrier may be required to keep people from crowding and to allow more people a view.

Preparation and Procedure

- Collect the necessary materials and equipment and select a suitable site.
- Practice techniques beforehand.
- Explain purpose and objective, then carry out demonstration.
- Invite audience to practice the techniques under guidance.
- Volunteers are tested to see whether they have acquired the demonstrated skill.

Hints

- To demonstrate effectively, you must be familiar with your equipment and skilled in using it.
- Make sure the audience fully appreciates the purpose of your demonstration—a visual aid can be used to reinforce your words.

- The easiest way to a successful demonstration is to build on individual experiences.
- Students practice best on their own time, without too many observers—some get very nervous while others are watching and criticizing.
- Practice, practice, and more practice is the rule for mastering a complicated procedure.

DISCUSSION GROUP

Two or more persons who come together to talk informally and to deliberate on a topic of mutual concern. Experiences are shared, opinions expressed, alternatives discussed, and action is planned. Interaction between individual members or between similar groups may provide the catalyst for problem solving and for effective planning.

Uses

- To identify, explore, and seek out solutions to problems.
- To develop plans for action.
- Where necessary, to change attitudes through an amicable examination of the evidence.
- To develop leadership skills.
- As a supplementary technique in many types of training.

Advantages

- Such a group pools experiences, abilities, and knowledge in order to reach recognized goals.
- Should provide for the full participation of every member.
- Can establish a democratic consensus.
- Can stimulate a desire to learn and to share.

Limitations

- Can be time consuming, particularly if persons with strong convictions or widely different backgrounds are involved.

- Preliminary exercises are needed before serious group activity is possible.

Requirements

- See Chapter 6—Participative Training.

EXERCISE

A work assignment, designed to provide practice in a skill or technique. Useful to review skills already learned and as a basis for self-instructional learning.

Uses

- To demonstrate a skill or technique.
- To provide practice.
- To reinforce or test learning.
- To test initiative.
- To review already acquired skills.

Advantages

- Can promote familiarity with the real thing.
- Helps to build confidence or independence.
- Represents self-instructional learning.
- Can be used to provide a welcome break.
- Can help to develop initiative.

Limitations

- Worthwhile only when well planned and tested.
- Often requires a good deal of organizing.
- The degree of skill that is acquired must depend on the individual capabilities.

Requirements

• They depend on the type of exercise. An adequate work space and tools; a carefully planned appointment schedule; adequate travel and accommodation arrangements; and up-to-date maps may all be necessary.

Hints

• During a lengthy workshop, field exercises can provide a worthwhile break for both tutors and participants.
• Every exercise needs to be both challenging and relevant. For example, "Go and investigate the situation and prepare a report to the director. Produce your recommendations by [mention date]."
• The students must always be given clear instructions on what is expected of them and by when.
• Critical but helpful feedback is an essential part of any worthwhile exercise—and don't forget to praise.

EXHIBIT

Display of visual information—can comprise models, photographs, visuals, and/or the real thing, with varying amounts of detail.

Uses

• To reinforce a lecture.
• As information for a conference or a convention.
• As a training tool—students examine at their leisure the details, photographs, books, or whatever else is included.

Advantages

• Can be used a number of times.
• Can be adapted and updated to meet varying needs.
• Can be used to encourage participation, so that each individual learns at the most convenient time and at his/her own speed.
• Can involve hearing, touch, taste, and/or smell as well as sight.

Limitations

- Can be costly.
- Difficult to use effectively with a large group.
- Needs ample space and a suitable, well-lit environment.
- May be expensive to pack and to transport.

Hints

- Make sure your exhibit is designed and arranged for clear visibility.
- Keep the message simple and clear—most exhibits are overcrowded with too much writing.
- Four basic rules for a successful exhibit are:

  1. First catch your audience's attention with a gimmick.
  2. Try to get each member involved.
  3. Tell them your message.
  4. To those who show interest, give a handout with further details, including where to go for more information.

- Every exhibit should look fresh and interesting.
- An active exhibit with living things moving or machines at work, or with a tape-slide or video demonstration, will attract the most attention.

FILM

Audiovisual, often detailed presentation of a subject, directed by one or more experts.

Uses

- To present factual material in a direct, logical manner.
- To provide a break in a training program.
- To show things not readily accessible to the individual viewer or the naked eye.
- To give a time sequence (seasons, for example).

- To arouse or increase interest.
- To illustrate various points of view.

Advantages

- Tells exactly the same story each time it is shown.
- Suitable for a wide range of subjects.
- Can easily be repeated.
- Its running time is known (or is easy to find out).

Limitations

- Is costly to make or buy.
- It can be difficult to find a film on a suitable topic at the right level for your particular audience.
- The film producer takes over control of your audience.
- No one can talk back to a film—it's one-way communication.
- Some trainers rely too heavily on the film.
- Requires expensive equipment and a degree of expertise.

Requirements

- Apart from the film(s), a projector that works and a screen are essential.
- A darkened room for showing.
- A qualified operator.
- A power source.
- Everybody must be able to see and hear.

Preparation and Procedure

- Set up and check the equipment in a room that can be darkened at the appropriate time (sun shining on a curtain can interfere with a blackout).
- Thread the projector and run the film through beforehand to make sure there are no breaks and that you can work the machine; also, to get the sound levels right (but remember that

the acoustics of a full room necessitate more volume than an empty room).

- Be sure to rewind and rethread the film so that it is ready for showing.
- Rewind the film after the final showing, before you return it to its canister.

Hints

- Wind the power cord around the leg of the table so that any late arrivers who trip on the cord in the dark don't pull the projector onto the floor.
- Arouse audience interest in the film by individual and group assignments.
- Test the audience after the showing to see how much has been learned—a rerun may be worthwhile.
- Select carefully the time you show a film—not right after a heavy meal, for example.

FORUM

A public assembly in which everyone is given a chance to voice his/her views.

Uses

- Can be an orderly discussion after a topic has been introduced by a speaker, a panel, or a film, or in some similar way.
- Can help to gauge public opinion on a controversial issue (the introduction of new legislation, for example).

Advantages

- Allows audience members to participate (even in a large meeting).
- Helps to develop a group opinion by testing ideas.
- Can also contribute to the idea development that must precede group action.

Limitations

- Its success depends on the ability of the chairman and the attitude of the audience.
- Heated debates may be stimulating but can delay the arrival at a consensus.
- Can get out of control when the topic is controversial and pressure groups get organized.
- Expert acoustic advice and equipment are necessary for large meetings.

Requirements

- An adequate hall or auditorium is necessary, depending on the numbers.
- Every member of the audience must be able to hear the speaker. At a large meeting, therefore, the speakers must come to a microphone or be within range of a "gun" microphone or a transmitting microphone.
- A capable chairman and (if necessary) assistants.

Procedure

- One or more speakers introduce and develop the subject.
- The chairman calls for questions or comments from the audience.
- The chairman immediately repeats each question asked from the floor and directs it to the appropriate authority.
- The chairman maintains control and sees that all the comments from the floor are relevant and brief—it is a good idea to summarize the arguments from time to time.
- The final summary, leading up to the conclusions that were reached, is also best done by the chairman or by a selected reporter.

Hints

- The chairman must be seen to be fair in maintaining control and must have a good sense of humor.

- It is wise to insist on "One question at a time please, and keep your comments brief." (The comments and the questions very easily get mixed up.)
- Assistants who are stationed in strategic locations in the audience can help to identify the people who want to speak and can hold the transmitting microphones.
- Questions and comments are most easily recorded (for "proceedings") by reporters summarizing them into portable tape recorders—few people can ask a clear question and few speakers can give an exact answer.
- When the audience is very large you should call for clearly printed questions and have a large box on the front of the stage or in the foyer to receive them.

GAMES AND SIMULATIONS

A *game* is a structured activity in which participants observe set rules and compete to achieve an objective.

A *simulation* is a training activity designed to mirror an actual situation (e.g., role-playing and in-basket exercises).

Uses

- To get trainees involved so they learn by doing.
- To encourage peer learning and show trainees that the group is a good learning resource.
- To review learning.
- To teach problem-solving and decision-making skills.

Advantages

- Involves groups and can be fun.
- Teaches skills quickly.
- An efficient substitute for reality.
- Adds variety and makes training more interesting.
- Allows risk taking in a safe atmosphere.
- Can provide a change in pace in a training program.

Limitations

- Some people dislike competitions. Be careful that the competitiveness of a game does not dominate the learning experience.
- A game models reality, but no game or simulation is truly realistic.
- A game or simulation can be expensive in time and money to build or buy. (The design and testing of computer programs can be costly.)

Requirements

- Competitive groups should be balanced in terms of experience and skills.
- Simple, clear, written rules and directions.
- A number of small meeting rooms for groups.
- Time limitations and deadlines.
- Equipment such as computers, reference materials, forms, or cards as required.
- Possibly recording and support services.
- A constructive debriefing session to analyze the game and explain its practical work applications.

Preparation and Procedure

- Test the game thoroughly to remove any bugs.
- Make sure the equipment is suitable for the groups and fully tested. If you use computers, will participants be able to use the program supplied?
- Decide on the best time in your training program to introduce the game.
- Explain the game.
- Check to see if the written instructions are understood by all participants.
- Divide the trainees into well-balanced groups so there will be keen competition.
- Arrange for assistants or observers for each group, if needed.
- Remind groups of approaching deadlines.

- Allow plenty of time for analysis of the game.
- At the debriefing, evaluate the exercise fully.

Hints

- Provide conditions in which participants can have fun while they learn.
- The more you involve your trainees, the more they will remember.
- Allow plenty of time—don't rush games.
- Simulations should be designed using real, current examples.
- Provide opportunity for the groups to evaluate their own performance after the final analysis.
- Rewards and prizes can add fun and motivation to a game.

A simulation game can be like a party: interesting to read about, but much more interesting to participate in.

GENERATING IDEAS (BRAINSTORMING)

The unrestrained offering of ideas by all members of a group where members put forward every conceivable idea (practicable and impracticable) on a subject.

"Let me ask you how many seeds there are in this apple I'm holding. Let's count them. There are eight. Now let me ask you how many potential apples there are in any one of these apple seeds. We've no way of counting that. The same is true of our group. We may know how many people are in our group, but the total of their ideas is difficult to determine." Brainstorming is a technique for estimating this.

Uses

- As a pre-evaluation discussion, to produce as many new ideas as possible—quantity before quality.
- To encourage practical minds to think "quantitatively," beyond day-to-day problems, rather than "qualitatively."
- To make progress on a problem when the more conventional techniques have failed.
- To develop creative thinking.

Advantages

- Often produces a solution to a previously insoluble problem.
- Many people are encouraged by the freedom of expression offered by this technique.
- Everybody can contribute and participate.

Limitations

- Many people have difficulty in getting started, away from practicalities.
- Many of the suggestions that are made may be worthless.
- In setting priorities in the evaluation session, other people's ideas must be criticized (but make sure it is done constructively).

Requirements

- Comfortable, distraction-free environment.
- An enthusiastic, skillful leader.
- One or more recorders to write up (on a chalkboard, an overhead projector, or a large paper pad) the ideas that are generated.
- Where possible, a semicircular seating arrangement.

Preparation and Procedure

- The leader plays the important role of catalyst, explaining the rules and stimulating the group members. A good warming-up exercise is to produce some common object such as a brick, and to ask each person to write down a list of all possible uses for it. Arrange a competition. After a set time (say, 10 minutes), find out who has the longest list and ask its compiler to read it out. Then call for any ideas that have not already been mentioned. Repeat the exercise with a variety of objects, until every member can produce a flow of ideas on any subject. By then, the group will have been warmed up for a real situation.
- The leader should explain the procedure and the recorders should be selected and briefed.
- As the ideas are called out, they are written down for everyone to see.

The greater their number, the better the chance of coming up with a solution.

Don't allow interruptions or criticism, but look for ways to combine or improve ideas.

Freewheeling, wild ideas are to be encouraged—it is easier to tone down than to think up ideas.

- Take a break as soon as the enthusiasm starts to fail.
- Examine each idea—does it have any practical application for our problem?
- Encourage each group member to pick out the best solution. Then compare and discuss the suggestions.

Hints

- Set deadlines—once your group is responding, work under pressure for limited periods only (not more than 45 minutes, but preferably less).
- If the group cannot get started, take a short break and start again.
- Group work should arouse friendly rivalry and stimulate the flow of ideas—advance notice of the discussion topic should get people thinking about it beforehand, perhaps overnight.
- A group that starts to go stale or some of whose members are inhibited should be broken up and sent off for a limited time to discuss the topic in pairs.
- Keep the groups small—up to eight members, including the leader and the recorders.
- Encourage small groups to compete for the best solution (competition is a great stimulus).

Five-Step Problem Solver

1. Define—make sure each member understands and agrees on the nature of the problem.
2. List its causes—encourage "lateral" thinking.
3. Brainstorm for possible solutions.
4. Choose the best suggestion—discuss and, if necessary, discard, examining every idea for an immediate or future application.
5. Plan the action (how to implement the chosen suggestion).

INTERVIEW

Meeting of two or more people face to face, usually for the purpose of questioning and examining one of them.

Uses

- To explore a topic in some depth.
- Can provide an informal approach.
- Can be a good way to handle a controversial issue.

Advantages

- Less formal than a lecture.
- Can be made more interesting than a lecture.
- The audience is represented by the interviewer(s).

Limitations

- The audience's role is passive.
- The interviewer must be skilled and must have done his/her homework.
- Talking to an interviewer in front of an audience can be daunting.
- Needs people who can relate well (and with, preferably, a sense of humor).

Requirements

- Comfortable seating.
- Good acoustics—everybody must be able to see and hear.
- A stage large enough to hold performers, microphones, and amplifying equipment.

Preparation and Procedure

- A meeting between the interviewer and an appropriate expert is arranged—ground rules, topics, line of questioning, and physical requirements (taking account of type and size of audience) are set.

- Set up the hall (stage, seating, lighting, and sound system).
- When the time arrives, the chairman introduces the topic, the expert, and the interviewer.
- The interviewer asks questions designed to explore and to develop the topic.
- Questions from the audience may be taken at the end.
- The chairman sums up the discussion (perhaps calling for the vote of thanks from the audience).

Hints

- The style of the interview is determined by the knowledge and the personality of the performers—a relaxed, informally probing interview is best.
- The interviewer must select each question carefully—repeating it in a slightly different form will help to make sure that each member of the audience has heard it.
- As well as putting the carefully prepared questions, the interviewer needs to be able to improvise apposite questions as the occasion arises.
- The expert should be set at ease before the interviewer moves on to the more difficult questions.
- The interviewer who has the ability to do so can also act as chairman.

LECTURE (SPEECH)

A usually carefully prepared, rather formal dissertation by one with claims to be an expert on the particular theme.

Uses

- To present factual material in a logical sequence.
- To present one or more points of view on a controversial subject.
- To recount personal experiences.
- To entertain or arouse an audience.
- To call for action.
- To stimulate thought, thus opening up a subject for discussion and further study.

Advantages

- Suitable for an audience of any size.
- Easy to organize.
- Some people learn more easily listening than reading.
- Simple recall exercises make its effectiveness easy to assess.

Limitations

- The audience's role is passive.
- There is a one-way flow of information.
- Efficient listening demands concentration.
- The lecture is the traditional, but very ineffective, method of imparting skills.
- Audience feedback is limited.
- The expert is not always a good speaker.
- Good speakers can be hard to find.

Requirements

- Speaker must be visible to, and heard by, the chairman and every member of the audience.
- Stage or raised platform (speakers' rostrum) with microphone, amplifiers, and loudspeakers when size of audience requires them.
- Visual aids (projector and screen) when called for by speaker.

Procedure

- The chairman introduces the speaker, with a brief statement of his/her qualifications and expertise in the selected topic.
- The chairman should ensure the speaker is given a fair hearing in the best possible conditions.
- At the end of the speech, the chairman (with the speaker's prior consent) should call for questions or points for discussion.
- Finally, the chairman should call upon a member of the audience to make a brief speech of thanks to the speaker.

Hints

- The effectiveness of a speech can be improved by encouraging the audience to take notes.
- Use visual aids as lecturer's "signposts" or memory joggers. Remember, a good picture is worth a thousand words.
- Make good use of stories, anecdotes, and other figures of speech to illustrate your points.
- Introduce devices such as repetition to heighten drama.
- Review and summarize regularly. "Tell them what you are going to tell them, tell it to them, then tell them what you have just told them."
- Be careful not to cram too many points in a single lecture.
- Give out copies summarizing your speech at its conclusion.
- Prepare your audience for selective listening. "We will try to find out tomorrow how much you have learned today."

Keep in mind the fleeting nature of oral communication.

LISTENING TEAM

Its members listen to the speakers, take notes, and question or summarize at the close (unlike the reaction team, they do not interrupt), thus providing interaction between the speaker(s) and a large audience.

Uses

- To take notes and to question a formal speaker or the symposium participants.
- To listen to, evaluate, and question a speaker (or group of speakers) in formal or informal discussions.

Advantages

- The audience is represented in a formal way.
- The team identifies and clarifies the issues, questions, and opinions developed by the speaker(s).
- A summary at the end will aid audience recall and help to avoid confusion.

Limitations

- When the team is being selected, the views of the majority of the audience need to be kept in mind.
- Each member needs to be knowledgeable on the subject, and should have no known biases.

Requirements

- Sufficient comfortable seats, arranged so that everybody in the audience can hear and see the speakers and the listening team.
- A stage or platform large enough for everybody who needs to be on it.
- Seats, a table, and lighting for the listening team.
- Microphones and an amplifying system powerful enough to allow the speaker(s) to be heard by everybody.

Preparation and Procedure

- Inform the speaker(s) beforehand about the team.
- Select the team, instruct it on its role, and introduce it to the speaker(s), with whom it should spend some time informally getting acquainted.
- The audience is told of the team and its function is explained.
- During the speech(es) the team members take notes and prepare questions and summaries.
- The team reports.
- The chairman sums up.

Hints

- Be sure to gain the prior approval of the speaker(s) to the use of this technique.
- Take care in selecting the team not to pick any member with a political axe to grind.

- Make sure you brief each party well, so that everybody knows precisely what is required of them.

MULTIMEDIA PACKAGE

A packaged set of teaching materials on a specific topic, designed for self-teaching.

Some packages consist of filmstrips or slides or a tape-slide presentation, a programmed workbook, discussion questions, reference papers, and copies of articles. With computers, trainees can instantly call up sections of text, video, pictures, maps, charts, narration, discussion, or music.

With multimedia systems, trainees get knowledge on demand. If you plan a good package to involve trainees as much as possible and challenge them with exercises, you will make learning exciting, stimulating, and more effective.

Uses

- Adaptable to any technical subject.
- Suitable for most self-learning situations.
- Suitable for distance learning.
- Suitable for automated group learning.

Advantages

- Does not require a tutor.
- Materials are carefully selected, and the package is specifically designed so it can be thoroughly tested before being used on a large scale.
- Learning is precise, and degree of accomplishment can be measured.

Limitations

- It is inflexible.
- It is expensive to prepare.
- Its packaging and postage can be expensive.

Requirements

- Audiovisual or computer facilities to produce it.
- A suitable package to contain it or a compatible computer disk suitable for the student's personal computer.
- A quiet study room.

Procedure

- The learning package is divided into modules.

  Read the instructions.

  Work through the module quickly.

  Listen to the tapes and view the slides.

  Read the references.

  Work through the module thoroughly.

  Complete the workbook or computer module.

- Afterward it is useful for the learners to come together in small groups in order to answer questions or to discuss problems or questions that are raised.
- Finally, the answers should be checked and the slides and references viewed again.

Hints

- Use this technique to bring busy professional people up to date with specific technical literature.
- The packages don't have to be expensive or complicated— start with a box file, photocopy the current literature, add a set of slides, prepare a work plan and apposite questions, add a voice tape from an authority on the subject, and you are in business.
- The technique works best when the individual is allowed to proceed at his/her own pace and afterward take part in a small discussion group to share experiences.

PANEL

A group of (usually) three to five specially knowledgeable persons, in full view of an audience, holding an orderly conversation on a set topic. (Differs from a symposium in that, after sometimes making a short, formal statement, the panel members talk only to one another.)

Uses

- To identify and explore a topic, issue, or problem.
- To weigh up the pros and cons of a course of action.
- To assist the audience in understanding a complex issue.

Advantages

- Frequent changes of speaker and viewpoint should maintain a high interest level.
- Can be very relaxed and informal and thus establish a favorable audience reaction.
- If you select the panel members carefully, all sides of an argument can be presented.

Limitations

- A skilled chairman is essential.
- Panel members need to be selected for balance and for their ability to communicate—any extreme differences of opinion may block progress toward a solution.
- The subject is not necessarily considered in a logical order.

Requirements

- Each speaker must be audible and visible to every member of the audience.
- A good stage setting, together with adequate microphones (if need be), and a satisfactory sound system.

Preparation and Procedure

- Organizer sets a clear objective.
- Panel members are selected and briefed.
- Meeting is held to discuss the objective and the ground rules.
- Program and publicity are printed and distributed.
- The stage is set, the sound system is tested, and sufficient seats are set out.
- Audience assembles and chairman briefly introduces the topic and the panel (stating their qualifications).
- Each panel member may make a brief formal statement (usually 5 to 10 minutes) setting out his/her point of view before the exchange of ideas and comments.
- May be followed by a forum to broaden the discussion and to involve the audience. (Agreement to this needs to be obtained beforehand from the panel members.)

Hints

- Take care in selecting your chairman and the panel members— the extrovert and the good communicator are needed.
- It is a good idea to explain the ground rules to the audience beforehand.
- The good chairman presents a balanced picture and makes sure that each member of the panel becomes involved—that the questions are shared about.
- The group chairman will try to relax the panel members and to maintain a sense of humor.
- On many such occasions, a summary by the chairman or the tutor is a good way to conclude the discussion.
- Don't forget to arrange for a vote of thanks from the floor to the chairman and the panel—and for formal thank-you letters to everybody after the event.

PEER TEACHING
(Peer-Assisted Learning or Peer-Mediated Instruction)

Small groups of peers act as both teacher and learner by switching roles (differs from peer tutoring, in which a student who is gifted in a subject helps another who is having difficulty in it).

Uses

- To break up a large class into small "learning cells."
- To reduce anxiety levels at the start of a training course by involving the whole class in an active learning process.
- To explore some particular subject in greater depth than the rest.

Advantages

- A one-to-one situation.
- Provides an active learning system for large lecture classes.
- Reduces student feelings of isolation and boredom.
- Gives the students greater responsibility for their own learning.
- Provides immediate feedback (for self-evaluating).

Limitations

- Peers are seldom experts in a subject and are not trained teachers.
- They are easily sidetracked by being asked irrelevant questions.
- The class as a whole may have difficulty in concentrating because of the noise being made by the groups.
- The student may feel antipathy toward his/her partner or at the idea of what is a highly structured method of studying.
- Progress can be impeded if competition among the groups becomes too strong.

Requirements

- Ample space.
- A quiet, sound-proof room.

Procedure

- Brief the class on the technique and its requirements.
- Break up the class into pairs or groups of three (triads).

- Each student must be called upon to gain experience in both the teaching and the learning roles. Each member of every group shares in asking the questions on a common reading assignment or on some other prepared assignment or set topic.
- The tutor is always available to supervise, to help solve problems or settle arguments, and to advise when necessary.
- The tutor should run a concluding session for the full class to attempt to answer any questions that came to light in the learning cells.

Hints

- Peer teaching can be a valuable technique and is well worth trying in a variety of situations.
- Most of the people in a large group are usually sitting next to friends. This tends to make peer teaching easier to get started than it might otherwise be.
- If the room is inadequate, send the class outside for half an hour to walk or sit in pairs, working on the planned assignment (perhaps over a cup of coffee).
- After paired discussion on a topic, any knowledge gaps should have become apparent. They should form the basis of questions to one of the resource persons.

PROGRAMMED INSTRUCTION

Material presented in any one or more of a variety of ways (texts, tape-slides, multimedia, or a teaching machine or computer) as a series of small, carefully graduated, sequential steps, the mastering of which requires the active participation of the learner at his/her own preferred pace (self-paced learning).

Uses

- For learning at a distance, by correspondence (particularly for adults, in their own home).
- Ideal for in-service training. Students come to a central training unit on their own time to work on a learning unit.
- As a break from more formal training.

Advantages

- Is as effective as conventional methods, and sometimes faster.
- Students do their own marking.
- Self-testing produces immediate feedback.
- Students themselves identify areas that require further study.
- In step-by-step study, the learner acts as his/her own pacesetter.

Limitations

- Developing and pretesting of programs can be costly in both time and money.
- There is a shortage of programmed-learning material.
- Too many students will lead to competition for the machines (computer, tape-slide machine, and so on).
- Most students tend to prefer more sociable learning systems.
- The inflexibility of what is a highly structured method.

Requirement

- The student must have a private quiet area in his/her accommodation or in the training area.

Procedure

- A learning package is divided up into units or modules.
- The student is required to follow instructions that are based on the media being used.
- Reinforcing exercises are set.
- Each set of work is marked before the student is allowed to proceed.

Hints

- The most effective learning occurs from challenging, stimulating, encouraging exercises—variety is the key to teaching and to learning.

- Programmed learning can be boring, or it can be fun—make sure it is also challenging.
- Programmed learning can be very encouraging for slow learners.
- Don't make the learning units too small—students will grow bored.
- If possible, make the learning machines available outside working hours to encourage their use.

QUESTION TIME

An organized session that follows formal speeches or a forum or panel. Members of the audience are invited to submit to the speakers any questions they may have.

Uses

- To clarify points made during the more formal sessions.
- To amplify points that were not fully covered.
- To seek new information.
- To involve the audience more closely.

Advantages

- Provides feedback to the speaker(s).
- Stimulates greater audience interest in the topic.
- Encourages more careful listening.
- It is psychologically sound for audience members to know they are able to participate, but do not have to do so.

Limitations

- At the close of a long session the audience may be weary.
- Time usually limits the number of questions.
- Physically difficult to handle in a large audience.
- Can be taken over by a few vocal members.
- Most members are too shy to participate.

Requirement

- Every member of the audience must be able to see and hear the questioners and to hear the answers.

Procedure

- The chairman sets the ground rules: "One question at a time, please, and keep your questions short and to the point."
- The chairman should repeat each question that is asked so that everybody can hear it (and to give the speaker time to sort out a reply).
- The chairman should also identify each questioner (by name, if possible) and ration out the time that is available.
- Finally, it is the chairman who keeps control, comments when necessary, sums up, and keeps the meeting running on time.

Hints

- The success of such an exercise depends largely on the experience and ability of the chairman—not only in keeping the audience under control and in good humor, but also in seeing that the answers given by the speaker(s) are to the point and as complete as possible.
- In a large audience, transmitting or gun microphones may be needed (the chairman may have spotters in the audience to assist him/her, or the questioners can be asked beforehand to come up to a centrally placed microphone).
- Audience members can be asked to hand in written questions during breaks, but make sure they are printed questions so the chairman can read them easily.
- If a large number of questions are received, a preliminary sorting should ensure that only the more appropriate ones are used.
- One or more containers can be placed around the room for written questions.
- If insufficient questions are forthcoming, call for a five-minute break and ask each audience member to combine with his/her neighbor in thinking up a question—that method usually works.

ROLE-PLAYING AND DRAMA SPOTS

A real-life situation (but with no script and no set dialogue) is improvised and acted out in front of the group, which then discusses the
implications of the performance for the situation under consider-
ation.

Uses

- To examine a problem in human relationships—for example,
  an extension worker or a social worker who is required to deal
  with a difficult client.
- To seek out possible solutions to an emotion-laden problem.
- To provide a group with insight into attitudes that differ sharply
  from their own.
- To practice new skills.

Advantages

- An effective way of stimulating discussion that is aimed at
  problem solving.
- Gives the actor a chance to assume the personality of (to think
  and act like) another human being, which should lead to a
  better understanding of the other person's point of view.
- Can be an effective means of avoiding the real-life dangers of
  the trial-and-error approach.
- Can add variety, drama, and fun to a formal training program.
- The actors are sometimes able to explain cultural differences
  simply and clearly.

Limitations

- Some people are too timid or self-conscious to act a role
  successfully.
- Role-playing loses some of its effect when the audience is too
  large.

Requirements

- Each member of the audience must be able to see the action.

- Actors seem to prefer being against a wall or on a stage, away from their audience.

Procedure

- The group leader must clearly define the situation (set the scene) before the role-playing begins.
- Role-playing can be introduced without any warning, but it is better to give the actors a little time to get used to the idea—they will then sometimes produce a very polished performance.
- The tutor should set a time limit beforehand: "You have 10 minutes in which to get your message across."
- After the first performance has been discussed, it is sometimes worthwhile to have the scene replayed by a second set of actors.

Hints

- Role-playing early in a program will help to break down inhibitions.
- Select your actors carefully.
- Where possible, allow them adequate time to improvise their props and costumes.
- Encourage a light-hearted approach.
- Arrange for several role-playing sessions—try making the groups competitive.
- In multicultural groups, role-acting can be a useful means of helping to break down interracial prejudices and promote understanding.
- Role-playing is generally spontaneous, while the drama spot is usually rehearsed. There is an important area between the two in which guidelines are established but the dialogue is spontaneous.

SEMINAR

A group whose members may each be called upon to play a formal role during its one or more study sessions, held under the guidance of a recognized authority in the subject.

Use

- To study in depth under an expert.

Advantages

- Provides learning through sharing.
- An authority guides the discussion and thus promotes learning.
- A well-run seminar will cover detailed and systematic discussion, thorough investigation, and careful inquiry.

Limitations

- Often the right leader is difficult to find.
- Often, too, the members are not prepared to devote the necessary amounts of time and hard work to preparing and presenting the reports.
- The expert's presence may inhibit some of the members.
- Sometimes it is difficult to research the topics and locate the sources of some of the material.
- Members will not make equal contributions—some will play only a passive role.

Requirements

- A semicircular seating arrangement is needed to promote group discussion.
- A comfortable, relaxed atmosphere is important.
- There should be facilities for note taking and for preparing reports.
- Audiovisual equipment should also be available.

Preparation and Procedure

- Define the seminar's objectives.
- Circulate the publicity material (with program details, and background notes on the leading authority).
- The number of enrollees may have to be limited, depending on the popularity of the topic, the facilities that are available, and the wishes of the leader(s).

- A preliminary meeting should define the topic, lay down the ground rules, assign the various jobs to individuals or to working parties, and draw up reference lists.
- Reports should be presented at one or more special sessions, with any necessary visual aids available and adequate supplies of any written handouts.
- All the members should be encouraged to discuss the reports and question the reporters.
- The seminar should be followed by an adequate number of summarizing and evaluating sessions.

Hints

- Right from the start, the leader should aim at establishing a stimulating working climate and a relaxed atmosphere.
- Each member must be encouraged to participate to the fullest extent possible—involve anyone who is shy or reserved by asking them questions.
- The leader(s) should ensure that everyone who speaks keeps strictly to the topic under discussion—it is very easy to digress.
- Many topics are controversial—a balanced approach to them is desirable.
- The seminar's success will depend on thorough research, the quality of presentation, the skill of the questioners, and the extent to which each member becomes involved.

SHORT COURSE

One or more intensive training sessions on some specific subject.

Uses

- To bring members of a group up to date on new developments in their field of interest.
- To provide groups of selected individuals with additional training in specific areas.
- To introduce new thinking, new insights, and new directions.
- To build morale and a sense of team spirit.
- Gets people away from their work environment to think and plan in new surroundings.

Advantages

- Can be useful in changing attitudes.
- Can help to build a group into a special team.
- When attendance is voluntary, it helps identify persons with special interests.
- Provides great flexibility in scheduling.
- Once a clear objective has been set, the rate of progress can be geared to the various members' needs.
- Can be successful in a variety of locations.

Limitations

- People usually expect too much—the expectation rate is too high.
- Any conscripted members may not respond, while volunteers may not really need or profit from the training.
- The advance arrangements involve considerable work and a degree of expertise.
- The exact numbers who are to attend may not be known until the start of the course.

Requirements

- A cloistered environment away from the work site.
- A main meeting room and a number of smaller rooms for group work.
- Such audiovisual aids as an overhead projector, paper pads, and so on.

Preparation and Procedure

- The site(s) should be set up well in advance.
- Publicity and promotion must be planned to reach the type of applicant who is likely to profit. Try to find out their habits (and who their bosses are).
- Choose the course members well in advance. Provide a list of precourse reading if one is needed.

- Prepare a list of "need-to-know information" for the course members. See Chapter 5—Managing Training.
- Provide sessions that introduce a wide variety of training methods.
- Arrange for adequate evaluation and follow-up.

Hints

- Some reserve and uncertainty are evident whenever a group of people comes together. Try to build up their confidence quietly, without embarrassing anyone.
- Prepare a precise, factual objective. (Be sure to secure the members' agreement on the course objectives before you start.)
- Start off by setting ground rules and establishing a working relationship. "What time will we start? Can you all make it by eight o'clock? Right, eight o'clock it is—and we'll start every morning at the same time."
- Prepare a map of the accommodation and surroundings—a great deal of time can be lost in describing just where the toilets are or when the mail is likely to arrive.
- Remember to keep your program flexible—it's what the people want to know that's important.
- Be sure that every exercise is relevant.
- Arrange some social and team-building activities—a social committee can take charge of leisure. A system of fines for "misdemeanors" can help to amuse the group and provide a nucleus fund for prizes, rewards, and social events.
- Competing groups engender friendly rivalry and will usually enhance learning.
- Provide opportunities for group members to discover and explore any mutual interests.

SKIT

A short, rehearsed, humorous (often satirical) stage presentation involving two or more persons—can be used to gain audience response to a particular problem or situation or to promote group discussions. (Differs from role-playing in that it has a prepared and rehearsed script, while role-playing is impromptu).

Uses

- To introduce a topic for discussion.
- To highlight a situation.
- To depict a problem.

Advantages

- Requires the active participation of at least part of the group.
- Helps to relax if it is introduced early in a training program.
- "Personalizes" a situation and can lead to emotional involvement.
- Can lift a program by awakening a timely interest and stimulating discussion.

Limitations

- Can take considerable time and ingenuity to organize.
- Talented performers are essential.
- Plot needs to be restricted to a single, clear message.

Requirements

- Should be played on a stage or against a wall (to simplify props).
- Must be visible to every member of the audience.

Preparation and Procedure

- Sort out your objective.
- Write the script.
- Choose the actors.
- Brief each actor.
- Assemble any necessary props and costumes.
- Rehearse on site.
- Brief the audience on what will be expected of them following the performance.
- The actual performance takes place.

- A discussion period follows.
- Summarize and evaluate (but only if prearranged).

Hints

- Furniture and scenery shifts should be kept to a minimum.
- Ask the actors to write their own script and to forage for any properties they may need.
- Use the skit to illustrate varying approaches to a problem (before-and-after situations, for example).
- Can be used to depict class, racial, or worker-management problems.
- Can help to relieve any stresses of multiracial training. (Every group has some born actors who will help break down barriers and inhibitions.)
- Look for enthusiastic actors—never force anyone into a role that could cause him/her embarrassment.

SYMPOSIUM

A series of short (usually 5 to 25 minutes) prepared speeches by up to five authorities, covering various aspects of a subject—usually followed by an audience-involvement session in which the subject is opened up.

Uses

- To present new material concisely and logically.
- To present several differing views on one subject.
- To provide a just analysis of a controversial issue.
- To clarify conflicting aspects of a complex problem and to depict the relationships of the parts to the whole.

Advantages

- Provides for differing points of view.
- Time-limited speeches minimize digressions.
- Brief speeches help to maintain audience interest.

- A comprehensive coverage becomes possible.
- Greater sources are available to answer questions.

Limitations

- Must be run as a formal event.
- The audience does not normally participate until the final stages.

Requirements

- Every member of the audience must be able to see and hear in comfort.
- A stage and (possibly) loudspeakers may be needed for a large audience.

Procedure

- The chairman sets the scene and introduces each speaker with a few brief remarks.
- A short question period may follow each talk, or the questions may be reserved for a formal discussion period at the end.
- A period for the exchange of questions and comments between the speakers in addition to the audience's question time may be worthwhile.

Hints

- Balance the speakers well—try to arrange an informal meeting with them beforehand, so that they get to know one another.
- The chairman needs to keep a firm control on the meeting and to see that the questions are spread evenly between the speakers—otherwise, the last speaker tends to be questioned most often.
- A spread of arranged questions from the audience can help to present a balanced point of view.
- Asking a guest authority to sum up at the end of the discussion is a good technique to follow.

TELECONFERENCE (An Electronic Get-Together)

The term *teleconference* can be applied to an audioconference, videoconference, and audiographic conference. All three involve two-way electronic communication between two or more groups, or three or more individuals, in separate locations.

Audioconferencing has voice-only communications. It uses special audio terminals for groups of 10 or more and speakerphones for smaller groups.

Videoconferencing has voices with two-way motion pictures using video cameras and monitors.

Audiographic conferencing uses voices with still-frame images using a video camera, computer-enhanced graphics, and an electronic writing tablet for annotation, all displayed on a monitor.

Uses

- To share information and experiences.
- To build working relationships, independent of distance.
- To plan projects.
- To help solve problems. (I once heard a medical emergency in Alaska resolved by a team of Hawaiian specialists using a satellite link.)
- To teach people in isolated areas. (The U.S. Peacesat satellite has played a major teaching role in the Pacific.)

Advantages

- Can save resources, such as time and money, by not having to bring people together for meetings. With these savings, more frequent meetings are possible.
- Can get an immediate response to a developing situation such as a disease outbreak, a natural disaster, or a business crisis.
- Can be used to explore topical issues.
- Experts can advise field staff or people living in isolated areas.
- Can link branch personnel with a central office for regular meetings.

Limitations

- Turbulent atmospheric conditions or a faulty telephone line can cause poor reception.
- A high-priority local event can prevent an important person from taking part.
- For international teleconferences, common languages and common technical terms are needed. Watch out for accents, speed of talking, and local jargon.
- International time zones must be considered. Don't set up a meeting when it is 2 A.M. in another hemisphere!

Requirements

- A prepared agenda. This is very important, but don't be too ambitious. Keep to a simple agenda.
- A budget. Know how much money is available and how much you expect to spend.
- Special arrangements must be made with your local telecommunications department.
- A facsimile machine is essential as a support tool for all forms of teleconferencing.
- A quiet, disturbance-free room, with suitable telephone lines and equipment. The floor should be carpeted, and walls should be curtained or contain acoustic tiles. Watch out for noisy chairs and slide projectors. Slides or films are best projected through glass panels.
- One convener who organizes the teleconference and acts as facilitator. At each location there should be a meeting leader skilled in controlling groups. The convener brings these separate groups together.
- An extra telephone line in each location for technical control. In multilocation conferences, only one location should be responsible for reestablishing bad connections. Most problems are not technical but, rather, management. You must agree on who takes control if there are technical troubles. If you lose contact with one location and all the leaders complain to their local telephone operators, utter confusion can result.

The Convener's Checklist (Tick When Done)

1. Purpose. What do you expect to achieve? (Write down your objective—keep it simple.) [ ]
2. Who will participate? Decide on locations. [ ]
3. Who will be the leaders in each location? (Select reliable people who can work well with groups and get things done. They can decide on the number of participants at each location. Groups of four to eight are good for interaction.) [ ]
4. Negotiate proposed dates and a suitable time. (Check the international time zones.) [ ]
5. Negotiate the agenda. (Not too many agenda items.) [ ]
   - Time meeting will start.
   - Rules and procedures.
   - Introductions and purpose.
   - Agenda items (in priority order).
   - Summaries and reviews.
   - Follow-ups.
   - Time meeting will finish.
6. Are background papers and equipment needed? (Preliminary local planning meetings are helpful to fine-tune the agenda and select background papers. A facsimile machine and, often, a projector are needed.) [ ]
7. Do you want minutes or published proceedings following the meeting? (If so, you will need to appoint reporters and organize the production and distribution.) [ ]

Planning, preparation, and follow-up are the keys to a successful teleconference.

Hints

- The agenda should be negotiated well in advance of the meeting. The more specific the agenda, or the training, the more effective the meeting will be. Background papers should also be sent by facsimile well in advance of the meeting.

- Put a notice on the teleconference room door to stop interruptions, and instruct the telephone operators not to put calls through to participants during your teleconference.

- Explain the ground rules. Start with introductions.

- Tell all present they are expected to take part in discussions.

- Speak slowly and clearly—use basic English.
- Keep your messages concise and to the point. Don't give too many details. You can say, "I will send a copy of the report."
- Check to see whether your messages are being understood. Ask leading questions, such as "What will happen if you carry out my recommendations?" (*not* "Did you understand that?").
- The local facilitator's job is to involve the quiet—and control the dominant—speakers. Say, "What do Joe and Mary think about that idea? They've had experience working on this type of project last year."
- Make brief notes during the teleconference to keep track of the discussion, to get names right, and to jog your memory.
- Always plan a back-up system—for example, a set of handouts just in case the projector doesn't work.
- Minutes should be sent to each location by facsimile as soon as possible after the meeting with handouts or other training materials.
- If you are taking a vote, don't say, "All in favor say 'aye.'" Say, "Who disagrees with the proposition?"
- If action was agreed upon, the name or names of persons responsible for tasks should be included in the minutes. Be specific, give commitments, and list time and dates tasks are to be completed.

Involve the quiet and control the dominant.

VIDEO

An audiovisual tape-playing (professional or amateur) device.

Uses

- To present factual material by one or more experts.
- To depict participants' responses and activities.
- To replay films.

Advantages

- Can be used to involve an audience in building its own production.

- Once purchased, it produces films relatively cheaply.
- The tapes can be used many times.
- Television programs can be copied for showing in appropriate learning situations (but be aware of copyright restrictions).
- Ideal for showing individuals how they are performing.

Limitations

- High initial costs.
- The small screen is suitable only for small audiences (for large audiences, costly large screens are needed).
- Easy to use for rough-and-ready productions, but attaining a high technical standard becomes costly.
- Large television receivers are difficult to move around.
- Can be time consuming.

Requirements

- Television set, video recorder, camera(s), tripod(s), microphone(s), and tapes.
- Soundproof studio suitable for production and for showings.
- Camera and sound crews.
- Room in which everybody can watch the screen in comfort.

Preparation and Procedure

- Brief the actors.
- Plan the objectives and the sequences.
- Write the script and practice the more difficult scenes.
- Film and edit.
- Show the finished product.
- Discuss.
- Evaluate.

Hints

- The use of video to demonstrate a skill (speaking, for example) can be time consuming—show your examples, but allow the participants to evaluate their own performance on their own time.

- People can be taught production skills in groups. Get them to compete in making a short production, then invite each group in turn to introduce, demonstrate, and evaluate their effort, with an open discussion to follow each one.
- There is more to making a good film than just buying the equipment—talk to the experts before you start!
- Before you decide to buy any equipment, make sure it is compatible with what you already own.
- Do your homework well before you purchase—don't listen to the glib salesman!

Making a Training Video or Film

For a large audience.   If you are making a video or film to be used widely, or for sale, employ professional filmmakers. Use actors, sound technicians, a professional camera team, and processors. Most audiences expect high-quality productions because they are used to the standards set by television and film producers.

For a one-off production.   Get assistance from experienced people. Make sure you have a good producer and, if possible, use two cameras.

Time spent planning is essential.
- What is your objective?
- What are you trying to accomplish?
- Is a video or film the best method?
- How are you going to use it?
- Prepare an outline of your story.
- Plan your shots using a story board and cards. If you have no board, lay them out on a table or on the floor. Move them about to get them into a logical order.
- Plan a beginning to capture immediate attention.
- Make your subject as interesting as possible.
- Aim to entertain as well as educate.
- Repeat your message several ways.
- Plan a memorable conclusion.

Entertainment is vital. The essence of a video is entertainment. If a program lacks that vital strand of drama, human interest, humor, or tragedy, you will have trouble getting your training message across.

Look Your Best on Video or Film

Tips for men:

- If you are clean-shaven, have a shave just before filming.
- Dust bald spots or a shiny forehead with face powder.
- Wear lightweight clothes. Filming under lights is hot work.
- Don't wear dark colors, bold stripes, or white shirts.
- Pastel-colored shirts with plain ties are best.
- Make sure your clothes, shoes, and socks are complementary.
- Don't wear large rings or shiny chains.

Tips for women:

- Avoid hairstyles that hide the face.
- If you have a light complexion, use heavier makeup to accent facial features.
- Darken blonde or grey eyebrows.
- Wear lipstick of a light, clear color.
- Don't wear black or white clothes—greys, browns, and blues are good.
- Fitted outfits usually look best.
- Emphasize vertical lines for a slimming effect.
- Avoid necklines or hemlines that might cause discomfort or embarrassment.
- Wear clothes you feel good in. Dark shades on light sets, lighter shades on dark sets.
- Avoid excessive jewelry.

Filming Training Interviews

- Don't drink alcohol before you start—your viewers will be able to tell.
- If sitting, sit up straight.

- Don't look at the floor or ceiling for inspiration—look at your interviewer.
- Try for a strong start.
- Show enthusiasm—get excited. Be more animated than usual.
- Speak with confidence and authority. Be credible. Act your role.
- Speak naturally. Most people speak in thoughts, not in sentences.
- Answer questions briefly and honestly.
- Don't lose your temper under any circumstances. Try to retain your sense of humor even when you are provoked.
- Avoid speech mannerisms, especially jargon or cliches such as "at this point in time." Watch out for um's and ah's and other thinking noises.
- Your viewers will remember the overall impression you make rather than what you say. Sorry, but it's true!

VISIT, FIELD TRIP, OR TOUR

Characterized by a planned itinerary, usually of a predetermined length, during which a particular environment or past or present event is observed and studied.

Uses

- To relate theory to real problems.
- To study something that cannot be brought into a classroom.
- To stimulate interest and concern.
- To demonstrate a course of action in the field or in a work environment.
- To talk to workers in their working environment.
- To find out details of how things are done.
- To study foreign cultures or environments.

Advantages

- Seeing is more meaningful than hearing or reading alone—it becomes easier to relate to the real thing.

- A particular practice can be related to its environment.
- A team spirit can be fostered through participants becoming acquainted socially.
- Usually more enjoyable than classroom learning.
- Useful for competitive learning. "Each group will prepare a report on [state topic]".

Limitations

- Planning and organizing can be time consuming.
- Travel and accommodation are costly.
- Definite numbers are often difficult to estimate.
- Tight schedules are hard to maintain.
- Certain risks are always involved—injuries or sickness, for example.

Requirements

- A definite starting time and easily identifiable starting point.
- Detailed transport, accommodation, and catering arrangements.
- Maps, information handouts, and detailed programs for each stop.
- A final get-together to review the project.

Preparation and Procedure

- An organizer must plan in detail and contact every person and place that is to be visited.
- Schedules must be drawn up, and maps and handout material (or learning aids) prepared.
- Every member of the party must be well briefed on what they will see, the purpose of each visit, what will be expected of them, the amount of spare time that will be available, and the time of their return.
- After each stop, members should meet to review what they have seen and its significance to them.

Hints

- Whenever possible, someone should make a preliminary tour to check on the details and the timing.
- If a preliminary tour is not possible, check the schedules and preliminary plans and resolve any difficulties well beforehand by telephone, later confirming in writing whatever is agreed upon.
- Build in social activities to provide for recreation.
- No schedule should be too tight—always try to allow for the unexpected or the unpredictable.
- Make sure that each of the contact points is known by everybody who needs to know it.
- Don't take anything for granted—telephone ahead each night, to ensure that the arrangements still stand.
- The project can be made more meaningful by asking for a detailed report on it afterward—either individually or competitively, in groups.
- All members must be told what will be required of them before they set out.

WORKSHOP

Usually, a group that is in retreat from a common workplace or similar workplaces in order to share work-related common interests; to improve individual work performances; to extend knowledge through intensive study, research, and discussion; or to solve their work-related problems by sharing common experiences and knowledge.

Uses

- To identify, explore, and seek solutions to work-related problems.
- For in-depth study of a situation (background and social and philosophical implications).
- To plan for future activities.
- To build up a text or construct proceedings (trainer's manual, for example).
- To develop a working philosophy.

- As part of a convention or conference to study brief, related topics or problems.

Advantages

- Can assemble and take advantage of a great deal of experience.
- Designed for a high degree of participation.
- Allows for group-determined goals, plans, and recommendations.
- Competition between rival groups is possible.
- A well-run workshop maintains the interest and enthusiasm of its members.
- It will generate more ideas than any individual would produce alone, and will promote confidence in agreed-upon solutions.

Limitations

- Its organization and running are time-consuming.
- Requires a high staff-to-student ratio.
- Requires more space and equipment than normally needed for a lecture series.
- Its members must be willing and able to work independently and yet to cooperate closely.

Requirements

- A common meeting place, with additional rooms for workshops.
- Seats should be arranged in a semicircle (avoid theater-type seating).
- An adequate library and other resource materials are required for research.
- Audiovisual materials for recording ideas and reporting back to full groups (large paper pads or overlays are ideal for this—with the help of blue-tack or masking tape, you can paper a wall with the sheets and thus build up a complete story or compare a series of reports).

Preparation and Procedure

- Set clear objectives and goals.
- Planning—How big? When? Where? How long (half day, five weeks)?
- Should proceedings be recorded and published? Who would do the work? How and when would it be done?
- Try to ensure the members are selected for their potential contribution and their experience rather than for reasons of prestige or seniority.
- Check on the physical facilities and material requirements well in advance.
- Arrange for an adequate number of carefully chosen resource persons to be on hand.
- Draft the detailed timetable.
- Prepare the need-to-know information handout (for a residential workshop this should include the travel arrangements, details of the sleeping accommodation, the mail collection and delivery times, meal times, the whereabouts of the toilets, and similar details). See Chapter 5—Managing Training.
- Make sure someone is on hand to welcome each new arrival, to help anyone with problems, and to answer any queries that may arise.
- Follow up the workshop with a final evaluating and strengths-and-weaknesses session.

Hints

- Start with discussion in pairs, but get group discussions going as soon as possible.
- Printed workshop proceedings are worth the effort it takes to produce them—they reinforce the learning and will later provide a useful reference source.
- Democratic discipline should govern all the workshop activities. Draw up a "working contract" that sets out all necessary details. What time shall we start? Shall we set up a social committee? and so on.
- Although any program needs to be flexible, its timing must be carefully planned. (Allow for reporting back.) If there isn't enough time for every group's report, ask the nonreporting

groups for any ideas that have not already been covered—but remember that a strict time schedule is essential to enable as many groups as possible to participate. Appoint a timekeeper to sound a warning bell (striking a spoon against a cup will do if no bell is available) a minute or so before time is up, and another bell at full time.

- It often proves a good idea to invite the opening speaker to stress the importance of the workshop (select speaker and topic to provide a fresh perspective on members' work and responsibilities).
- Precise workshop goals and objectives should be approved and adopted on the first day.
- Foster competitiveness in setting up a group-reporting system—but make sure it is lighthearted rather than serious.

Little of what we passively listen to is remembered. The greater our involvement, the more we learn.

Chapter Nine

Visual Ways

Words alone are very ineffective as a means of teaching. However, by combining them with visual aids such as slides, diagrams, films, videos, models, and demonstrations, you can improve the effectiveness of your training. Use visual aids at every appropriate opportunity—they will add interest and variety to your presentation.

Seeing is discovering that something is possible.

THE REAL THING IS BEST

Visual aids need not be expensive. Often the simplest ones are the most effective. The best visual aid is the real thing, but simple models, charts, and overhead transparencies can save you much talking and reinforce your message.

I once attended a lecture where only one slide was used. It was projected onto a large screen as a backdrop for a lecture on erosion and was very effective.

Many organizations use computer graphic packages to prepare their presentations. Small laptop computers can be linked to overhead projectors—but remember, the more electronic your presentations, the greater the cost and the more things that can go wrong.

I once saw a Pulitzer prize winner embarrassingly refund the entrance money for his tape-slide lecture when his slide projectors got out of synchronization and he had to abandon his presentation.

A good visual aid can save you a lot of talking.

WHEN USING VISUAL AIDS

If you are using visual aids in your training, do your homework thoroughly.

You will know the size and composition of your audience and their level of knowledge on the subject. Plan and design your visual aids at the appropriate level for learning and large enough for all to see. Use your imagination when selecting visual aids.

If you have too much information for a good visual aid, prepare a printed handout.

- Check the room you will be using for training. Know where the power points and light switches are situated, and make sure the ones you are using are in working order.

- Check your equipment. Have a spare bulb for your projector handy and any tools you might need to change the bulb. Focus your projector.

- If you are using a screen, adjust the height so that people's heads will not obstruct the view of those sitting behind. Angle the screen if you are using an overhead projector to stop any "keystoning" effect.

- Check the blackout facilities. If you are speaking in the daytime, note the time of your presentations and whether the sun's rays will cause problems.

- Position the screen so you will not be standing in front of it.

- Check that there are no loose power cords to trip over. Tie loose cords to the leg of a table.

- Practice using your visual aids in the training room. Check for viewing and timing. Go to the back of the room to make sure your slides are easily seen.

- Arrive early before your presentation to make sure everything is still in order. Then relax!

- Enjoy yourself and your trainees should enjoy themselves too.

We learn best when we are having fun.

Appropriate Visual Aids for Each Job

There are three golden rules for visual aids:
Visual aids must be

Simple

Understood

Seen by all

The visual aids you choose will depend on the type of information you want to present, the size of the audience, and the venue. Your venue could be a small room, a large auditorium, or the great outdoors. They will also depend on the equipment and assistance available and whether it is possible to black out the room or hall.

Make sure the visual aids you choose are the best ones to illustrate your points. They must be the most suitable for the size of your audience and for your venue.

Are Your Visual Aids Suitable?

Visual Aid	Audience Size				Needs Dark Room	Needs Power Plug
	50	100	200	1,000		
Actual object	*	*	*	*	No	*
Chalkboard	Yes	No	No	No	No	No
Chart and display board	*	*	*	No	No	No
Comic strip and cartoon	*	No	No	No	No	No
Film	Yes	Yes	Yes	Yes	Yes	Yes
Flannelboard	Yes	No	No	No	No	No
Flip chart	Yes	No	No	No	No	No
Magnetboard	Yes	No	No	No	No	No
Model	Yes	*	*	No	No	*
Overhead projector	Yes	Yes	Yes	Yes	No	Yes
Poster	*	No	No	No	No	No
Slide (35mm)	Yes	Yes	Yes	Yes	Yes	Yes
Videotape and closed-circuit television	Yes	*	No	No	Yes	Yes
You	Yes	Yes	Yes	Yes	No	No

* Depends on circumstances

Always try to demonstrate with the real thing, if possible. It will be far more effective than any substitute. Also, an "active" visual aid such as a film or a working model will be more effective than anything passive such as a chart or a table of figures. The mere act of writing on a transparency or of rearranging the objects on a magnetboard will arouse more interest than a completely static, prepared chart or diagram.

Your choice of visual aid will depend on:

- The information you are trying to convey.
- The size of your audience.
- Where you are speaking.

- Whether it is possible to black out the room.
- What help you can get in preparing your visual aids.
- What type you like using best. If you feel comfortable using one kind, you will be more relaxed and convincing. But get used to the new types of visual aids and practice with them until you feel confident.

VISUAL AIDS

There are many types of visual aids. This section lists in alphabetical order some of the common ones with their advantages and disadvantages and practical hints when using them.

Chalkboard and whiteboard

Chart and display board

Comic strip and cartoon

Computer projection

Film

Flannelboard

Flip chart

Magnetboard

Model

Overhead transparency

Poster

35mm slide

Videotape and closed-circuit television

Be your own visual aid

Chalkboard and Whiteboard

Advantages

- Low cost.
- Allows use of color.
- Suitable for compiling lists.
- Good for building up a story.
- Good for illustrating a point during question time.

- An "active" visual (i.e., it involves movement with the speaker writing or drawing). This arouses interest and adds variety to the talk.

Disadvantages

- Chalkboards are dusty and dirty.
- You turn your back on your audience when you are writing— unless you prepare your board beforehand.
- You should clean or remove board before you move on to next point.
- Speakers often stand between their audience and the board.
- Unsuitable for a large audience because of its limited visibility.
- You need practice in drawing and printing clearly to use it well.

Tips

- Before you use a new chalkboard, fill its pores with chalk dust by patting entire surface with chalked duster—this prevents permanent impressions.
- Don't stand in front of the board—remember (as with other visual aids) practice improves performance.
- Prepare complicated diagrams before you start. Cover them and expose them when they are required.
- If possible, don't try to do complicated diagrams in front of your audience. If you must do so, use templates or a pencil to draw guidelines before you talk.
- Whiteboards are ideal for small meetings. They are not dusty like chalkboards and many can also be used as magnetboards. The pens tend to dry up and are more expensive than chalk.

Chart and Display Board

Advantages

- Give a brief visual message.
- Good for summarizing points.
- Can be prepared by a signwriter using good layout and color.

Disadvantages

• Often large and awkward to carry.
• Not suitable for large audiences.
• Must be removed before you go on to the next point in your talk or it is a distraction.

Tips

• Signwriters' calico is ideal for a portable chart, and poster paints are suitable for the lettering.
• For an audience of 40, a chart should be at least 55 cm by 70 cm.
• Most people can see 3-cm-high lettering from 10 m.
• Use no more than six or seven lines on a chart.
• Lettering must be thick. Exaggerate the spacing between letters and words.
• Your chart can be made into a "striptease" chart if you use thick paper or light card to cover the text or drawings. (Cellulose tape wound sticky side outward around two fingers held slightly apart gives a two-sided sticky surface to hold up the cover sheet.) Then you can expose your message gradually.

Comic Strip and Cartoon

Don't overlook the comic strip and the cartoon when you want to get a message across. Both of them, if used effectively, will attract attention and arouse interest. Their success depends on the ability and the imagination of the creator.

The comic strip aims to entertain by telling a story in a series of drawings. The story should be brief and packed with action. It should deal with an exciting or an amusing situation. Scripts should be brief and simple.

A well-designed comic can be a useful educational handout. Bright color can make it more effective.

The serious cartoon is often intended to influence public opinion by caricaturing a person, an idea, or a situation. The humorous cartoon is usually intended to amuse but can be used to convey a very serious message.

Advantages

- Almost universal appeal. (Most people are lazy readers but eager lookers.)
- Can attract both the literate and the illiterate.

Disadvantages

- A clever scriptwriter and artist are needed.
- The artist needs to fully understand the local scene and sense of humor.

Tips

A good cartoon:

- Deals with a single idea.
- Simplifies issues.
- Is well drawn.
- Has humor.
- Usually has only a brief caption.
- Can be readily understood by the target audience.

Computer Projection

Computer projection units combined with overhead projectors have revolutionized training. Vast amounts of data, visual aids such as

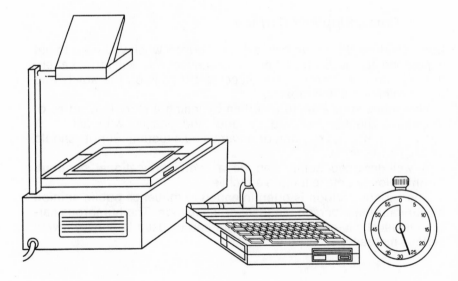

charts, maps, and diagrams, and voice, sound, and music can be stored in the computer and images projected on a large screen.

Advantages

- Multimedia color presentations add interest to training.
- Notebook or laptop computers are small, light, and easy to carry.
- The units are easy to set up and operate if trainers have computer skills.
- Notebook computers can hold large amounts of information (many hold up to 34,000 pages of text).
- All modern software programs (such as Windows) can be projected, if used on an IBM compatible computer, with an overhead projector.
- Programs can be stored on the internal hard disk. Additional information can be added using floppy or hard disks.
- Disks are easily mailed or couriered to users.
- Tutors or trainers can have their individual training programs on their own disks.
- Trainers can simulate or animate training situations on a large screen.
- Ideal for case studies as you can vary the options and study different combinations.
- Picture images are clear, and you can zoom in on important areas or use an electronic pen to highlight key issues.

Disadvantages

- The operator needs computing skills.
- The units are costly but will get cheaper.
- Because of their small size, they are liable to be misplaced or stolen if left unattended.
- Easy to drop or damage.

Tips

- Set up a menu on your computer to speed the selection of programs.
- Insure your unit in case it is dropped, knocked onto the floor, or stolen.
- Carry spare sets of batteries when traveling.

Film

Advantages

- Excellent for showing action and for demonstrating.
- Can condense or stretch time.
- Good for close-up demonstrations.
- Suitable for large audiences.
- Can reproduce the past for today's lessons.

Disadvantages

- Expensive to produce.
- Projectors are usually heavy and expensive.
- Some skill is required to set up and operate a projector.
- The film producer takes control of your meeting.

Tips

- A verbal introduction is helpful.
- Use your film (or part of it) to help illustrate a point—don't let the film take over completely.
- After a film, involve your audience. Use the screening as a means to stimulate worthwhile discussions. Ask questions. "Did you agree with . . . ? What did you like best about . . . ? What were the main points?"

Flannelboard

Advantages

- Cheap to make.
- Can be rolled up.
- An active visual (i.e., the speaker adds or rearranges objects to build up a story).

Disadvantages

- Not suitable for large audiences.
- Not as reliable as a magnetboard.
- Not suitable for outdoor use.

Tips

- Any rough-textured cloth such as flannel or blanket can be used. Pin it tightly and securely on a solid backing. (You can attach it to a chalkboard with spring clips.)
- The flannel should be a neutral color.
- Graphics should be prepared on stiff, light cardboard with sandpaper or rough-textured cloth stapled or glued lightly to the back. (Too much glue can mat the fibers and prevent the graphics from sticking to the flannelboard.)
- For heavy graphics or for outdoor demonstrations in windy conditions, use Velcro (two materials, one covered with hooks and the other with loops, which cling together).
- Write its name on the back of each piece. This saves time when assembling the whole graphic.
- Make sure your board is tilted slightly backward or your graphics may fall off.

Flip Chart

Advantages

- Readily available.
- Low cost.
- Easy to carry (roll them up).
- Easy to prepare using large colored crayons or thick felt pens.
- Can be prepared beforehand.
- You can "ghost write" details in pencil.
- As each sheet is finished, it is turned over so it does not remain as a distraction.
- It is easy to refer back to previous sheets.
- Can mask sections and strip off covers at appropriate times to reveal message.
- Sheets can sometimes be used again.
- They can be torn off and stuck to a wall with masking tape to build up a plan.

Disadvantages

- Suitable only for small audiences.
- Needs some type of easel support.

- The speaker turns away from audience to write on the pad or read from it.
- Some speakers stand in front of it.
- Unsuitable for outdoor use.

Tips

- Thick crayons are more reliable than felt pens.
- You can pin the pad to your lectern with thumb tacks. Drape the sheet with your visual aid in front of the lectern. You can have any notes you require written on the back of the next sheet. Drop that sheet over the lectern at the appropriate time to expose the next visual.
- Opaque white plastic can be used instead of paper and is more durable.

Magnetboard

Advantages

- Any iron or steel surface (such as a steel cabinet) can be used.
- Suitable for outdoor use.
- Good for television visuals if surface is dull.
- An active visual.

Disadvantages

- Heavy to transport.
- Graphics with magnets attached are time-consuming to prepare.

Tips

- Magnets can be either small pot, bar, or flexible plastic tape (containing embedded magnetic filings).
- Attach the magnetic strip to light card with glue, adhesive tape, or staples.
- A metal-gauze screen makes a lightweight magnetboard, but needs a rigid frame. A picture, map, or drawing can be mounted behind the screen for greater effect.

- Bottle tops make good "players" for showing sports-team movements on a magnetboard. Glue 2-cm pieces of plastic-strip magnet inside bottle tops which have been painted and numbered appropriately.

Model

There are several types of models: scale models, smaller or bigger than the original but in correct proportions; cut-away models, where pieces can be removed to reveal what is inside; build-up models, where pieces can be added to complete a model; and working models, powered by man, batteries, electricity, animals, etc.

Advantages

- Shows principles or characteristics when you cannot use the real thing.
- Can be smaller or bigger than the real thing; can also be simpler.
- Easy for most people to understand.
- Gets attention and fascinates some people, especially if it is a working model.

Disadvantages

- Often expensive to make.
- Often difficult to pack and transport.
- Rarely suitable for large audiences.

Tips

- It must be large enough and simple enough for everyone in the audience to see and understand.
- It must be accurate enough to be convincing.
- It should be strong and easily portable. Make sure you have good containers for transporting.
- A working model must be easy to operate and maintain.
- Remember, a model is usually a poor substitute for the real thing. If possible, demonstrate with the real thing.

Overhead Transparency

Advantages

- Can be used in a lighted room.
- You can maintain eye contact with your audience—you can write or draw as you talk.
- Active (like a chalkboard).
- Suitable for small or large audiences.
- Transparency can be prepared earlier, and by exposing a little at a time, you can build up a story.

Disadvantages

- Requires some operating skills.
- Screen should be angled 90 degrees from the projector's lens.
- Lamp is fragile.
- Can be bulky to transport.
- Heat from the lamp and the bright light can cause discomfort.
- If your writing or drawings are untidy, this will be accentuated on the screen.

Tips

- Ideally have no more than six lines of writing on a transparency or six words per line.
- Keep the lettering at least 6mm high.
- Most photocopying machines can be used to produce overhead transparencies, but you must use plain paper copier transparency film.
- Photocopying machines that enlarge can be used to make transparencies from text, cartoons, or drawings in publications.
- You may have to enlarge several times to get the correct size.
- If you clip and paste to make a visual, you will find a glue stick handy. You will not need to cover the edges of additions with white paint to stop them from showing on the transparency if you reduce the contrast on the photocopier.
- Some desktop publishing computers have graphics packages that enable you to make transparencies.

Poster

A poster is useful for getting a single important idea across quickly. It should have a strong eye appeal to attract attention.

Advantages

- Can be displayed for its artistic value as well as for its message.
- Can remain on display for lengthy periods.
- Can be transported easily and cheaply.
- Can be produced cheaply by silk screening.

Disadvantages

- Often costly to design.
- A big print run is needed to make glossy posters economic.
- Must be displayed where people have time to look at it.

Tips

- A good poster has:

    A simple message.
    Bold design.
    Bright colors.
    Brief, clear wording.

35mm Slide

Advantages

- Projectors are readily available at most venues.
- Slides are easy to carry and store.
- Easy to duplicate.
- Slides can be rearranged and others added to keep a series topical.
- Very small objects can be enlarged on a screen.
- Objects are shown in natural color.

- Speaker controls the speed so he or she can explain or answer questions if necessary.
- Suitable for large or small audiences.

Disadvantages

- Time consuming to prepare and process.
- If you have a projectionist, you must coordinate and practice your presentation.
- Needs blackout facilities.
- Speaker loses eye contact with audience during blackout.
- Rapid light changes are distracting.

Tips

- Aim for one idea per slide.
- Keep wording to a minimum.
- Add color to a black-and-white slide by backing it with a colored blank (in the same mount).
- Sort and label all your slides and arrange them in containers or carousels in logical order.
- Put a thumb spot on the lower left-hand corner of each slide. Slides are inserted in the projector upside down with the thumb spot at the right-hand corner.
- Arrange the room and seating, and check all equipment before your presentation.
- Have a test run to make sure the slides are in the correct order and none are upside down or back to front.
- When you set up your projector, always wrap the cord around the leg of the table it is placed on. Then if someone trips over the cord in the dark, the projector won't crash to the floor.
- Check that light from your lectern does not fall on the screen.
- Face your audience when you talk—not the screen!
- Don't leave a slide on for a long time. Most people will grasp important points in 15 seconds.
- If you want to talk between slides, slip in a blank pleasantly colored slide (easily made by photographing the sky or a colored card).
- Use a remote control attachment and set your own pace.

Rules for Using Slides and Tranparencies

- **One idea only.**
  Limit the amount of information on a transparency or slide to a single idea. Don't make several points on one visual aid.

- **Use title phrases.**
  Use clear, simple title phrases so the audience knows immediately what the visual is about; for example, "Gross Income," *not* "Chart No. 1."

- **Must be seen by all.**
  Make sure all visual aids can be seen clearly from the back and the corners of a room. Use the 6/6 rule—no more than six lines on a slide or transparency and six words per line.

  No more than 6 lines and 6 words per line.

- **Rehearse.**
  Have a rehearsal in the room you will be using. Anticipate problems. Check power points to see if they are live. Know the position of the switches. Check blackout facilities. Check the height and angle of the screen, so all the audience can see it with no heads in the way. If you are using an overhead projector, angle the screen. Make sure you have a spare bulb or that there is another projector available in an emergency.

- **Coordinate your talk and visual aids.**
  Show a visual aid only when you are talking about that topic.

- **Allow time.**
  Give your audience time to study each visual and allow yourself time to explain details, if necessary.

- **Switch off.**
  Keep your visual on the screen while the projector is turned on—don't blind your audience with white light. When you want to direct attention back to you, cover up the visual or turn the projector off.

- **Watch your audience.**
  Talk to your audience, *not* to your visual. Watch your audience to see if they are understanding your visual aid.

- **Not too many.**
  Don't overdo visual aids. Use a few good ones; too many are boring.

- **Handouts.**
  If people want additional information or details, give them handouts *after* you have finished talking.

- A projector can be used as an emergency spotlight to illuminate a speaker or a display.
- If you have to show slides to a small group in daylight you can make an emergency rear-projection screen from a cardboard box and greaseproof paper (not waxed paper).

How many slides will you show? This will depend on the nature of your talk and whether you are talking about the slides or using them only to illustrate certain points. *But don't use too many.*

- For a 20-minute talk, 10 slides is often adequate.
- Show only the best—leave out the rest.

Videotape and Closed-Circuit Television

Modern video cameras are very portable, easy to operate, and enable you to play colored videos almost instantly. Videotapes for educational purposes should be well planned and rehearsed, and produced by skilled cameras and sound technicians.

Advantages

- Captures an event so it can be replayed later, often at a more convenient time.
- Instant replay is possible.
- Can be replayed many times and stopped for discussions.
- Can show close-ups to a large audience.
- Can be used to magnify very small objects.
- Shows objects in natural color.
- Graphics, film clips, and slides can be inserted where appropriate.
- Outdated material can be edited out.
- People can watch themselves and evaluate their own performances.

Disadvantages

- Equipment is costly—particularly large screen projectors.
- Television sets for viewing are not readily portable.
- Support equipment needs to be compatible.

- Detailed planning is often necessary.
- Extra lighting is usually needed.
- Skilled camera and sound technicians and studio facilities are needed for quality productions.
- Production can be time consuming and costly.
- People are often critical of amateur productions because they are familiar with highly professional standards in cinemas and commercial television.

Tips

- When using graphics, don't use white card—black lettering on grey or light blue is best.
- Make graphics one-third wider than their height. Be careful that edges are not masked when reproduced on screen.
- Have no more than four or five lines of printing on each visual and try not to use more than 15 letters or spaces per line.
- See Chapter 7—Training Ways. The section on video has many helpful hints on making a training video.

BE YOUR OWN VISUAL AID

There is far more to training than the contents of your talks and exercises.

- When training, dress neatly but be comfortable. Wear clothes that are appropriate for the group you are training.
- The way you dress, the way you move, and the way you sound can help set up a climate conducive to learning.
- Try to develop a rapport with your group right from the start. Be enthusiastic; get them involved as soon as possible. Your facial expressions, the tone of your voice, your movements, and your gestures will all have impact.
- Make an extra effort to be enthusiastic—enthusiasm is contagious!
- Use your hands to illustrate movement and form. The volume, speed, and tone of your voice should reflect your emotions.
- You will catch and maintain attention if you pause occasionally. Speak distinctly without strain. If you have trouble projecting your voice, practice reading aloud. If necessary, seek advice from a speech teacher.

- Move naturally and confidently—be your normal self. Get your friends to mention any annoying mannerisms so you can make an effort to overcome them.

- Mime is a very effective, nonverbal form of communication. A shrug of the shoulders, a smile, a look of dejection can say more than words. Try practicing in front of a mirror or join a mime class.

- Don't be afraid to do a little acting or storytelling, especially if you can tell stories against yourself. A sense of humor is a valuable asset for all trainers.

- Enjoy yourself and your trainees should enjoy themselves too.

We learn best when we are having fun.

Chapter Ten

Now Evaluate Yourself: How Good Are You as a Trainer?

Tick if you believe you are doing a good job.

- Assess the general standard of learning and knowledge of your trainees so that you can begin at an appropriate level? [ ]
- Plan and develop every training program to suit the varied needs of the group members? [ ]
- Present well-organized sessions? [ ]
- State the objectives of training at the start? [ ]
- Explain any changes you intend to make and reasons for the changes? [ ]
- Make enthusiastic statements about the course and discuss expectations with participants? [ ]
- Involve participants in their learning right from the start? [ ]
- Start with a topic familiar to the group, but add something new to stimulate curiosity and arouse awareness of previously unrecognized needs? [ ]
- Move forward one step at a time? [ ]
- Adjust the size and difficulty of each step to the learners' abilities? [ ]
- Adjust each step, not only to the group as a whole but to individuals in the group? [ ]
- Build each step on the preceding step? [ ]
- Point out what was important to learn in each session? [ ]
- Give step-by-step instructions when needed— in writing? [ ]

- Make sure you provide opportunities for all members to practice their newly acquired skills?   [ ]
- Relate course materials to real-life situations?   [ ]
- Use relevant examples to help make points?   [ ]
- Set exercises that are worthwhile and relevant with useful practical recommendations?   [ ]
- Use a variety of teaching techniques?   [ ]
- Use a variety of teaching materials and different types of visual aids?   [ ]
- Summarize often?   [ ]
- Review at the start and the end of each session?   [ ]
- Set up challenging and competitive group situations?   [ ]
- Encourage unresponsive students to participate?   [ ]
- Make every member feel involved and feel they can share experiences freely without loss of face?   [ ]
- Initiate conversations with participants before and after sessions?   [ ]
- Address each person by name?   [ ]
- Praise students during sessions?   [ ]
- Encourage thinking and the use of imagination in your exercises?   [ ]
- Carry out simple recall exercises?   [ ]
- Allow sufficient time for creative thinking to produce worthwhile ideas?   [ ]
- Set challenging assignments?   [ ]
- Work students hard for specified periods, never for in-definite periods?   [ ]
- Set deadlines and keep to them?   [ ]
- Make written comments on exercises?   [ ]
- Encourage research and public reporting back to the group?   [ ]
- Encourage trainees to produce written summaries of their research and class proceedings or manuals.   [ ]
- Give brief, factual handouts?   [ ]
- Develop a working climate that encourages construc-tive self-criticism?   [ ]

- Carry out regular evaluations of:
  The course contents? [ ]
  The curriculum? [ ]
  Your effectiveness as a tutor? [ ]
- Keep up to date with new techniques and training tools by reading, researching, and attending seminars and training sessions? [ ]
- Experiment with new training methods. [ ]

Most teachers and trainers talk too much.

HOW CAN YOU IMPROVE?

Look at all the questions you have not checked. These are your training weaknesses. (Mark these with a highlight pen.) Make a real effort to work on these areas. Tackle them one at a time and plan how you can improve as a trainer.

1. Decide which one you will deal with first.
2. Make an action plan.
3. Start at your next training session.
4. Keep to your plan.
5. Evaluate your performance during sessions and at the end of each session. Don't look for an ego boost; look for ways to improve.
6. How can you do a better job next time? Examine your behavior, not yourself.
7. Keep trying.

Practice is the best master.

Glossary

This glossary will help you:

Read training books and periodicals with a greater knowledge and understanding.

Give simple definitions for many training terms.

Standardize training terms with your colleagues.

accountability The extent to which the results of a project, program, or activity can be justified to an organization in terms of operational goals and financial returns.

accountable Liable to be called to account; responsible.

accreditation The formal recognition that a trainer is capable of delivering training units to a specified standard.

action learning Learning through doing. Often used to describe a situation where students attend formal training, then return to the workplace to observe selected activities before returning for reporting and additional training.

action plan A plan designed to achieve a specific objective. It gives target dates and persons responsible for completing each activity and often sets out the budget. It is also known as a contract.

adoption The mental process through which an individual passes from first knowledge of an innovation to the actual use of it.

alter ego (Latin for *other self*) The observer watches a learner in a situation and gives feedback on the adequacy of the action.

appraisal Evaluation against expectations or the ideal performance. A systematic review of all aspects of a project, plan, or program.

aptitude The capacity of a person to acquire knowledge or skills.

assessment The process of collecting and interpreting evidence of learner competence or achievement.

assimilation The merging of groups or individuals into one group with a common culture and identity.

ASTD (American Society for Training and Development) The professional society for trainers, with headquarters in Washington, D.C.

behavior modeling Structured role-playing where students act out roles copying good examples.

belief A statement accepted by a person as true.

book reviewing An exercise where texts on the topic under study are reviewed by students to build up a class annotated reading list.

bottleneck A hindrance which causes students not to change their behavior in the direction desired by the trainer.

briefing Giving all the facts of a planned operation.

buddy training Working with a colleague who is competent in coaching.

buzz group A group working on an assigned task.

case study Comprehensive account of an event or series of related events. A technique designed to give group training in solving problems and making decisions by examining a specific case from a real work situation.

chaining A series of responses, each of which leads to the next.

change agent A person who seeks to influence the behavior of clients in a direction recommended by an employer.

chucking Arranging groups of words into meaningful segments to help memorization.

climate The mood in the training situation that may affect the outcome in a positive or negative way.

clinic Meeting(s) devoted to diagnosing and solving problems.

coaching Systematically increasing the ability and experience of an employee, student, or athlete by giving planned tasks with continuous appraisal and advice.

code Any system or group of standards (beliefs, rules, or laws) that regulates the behavior of group members.

cognition Thought processes concerned with problem solving, reasoning, perceiving, and language.

colloquy A formal conference. A modified version of a panel, where half are resource persons while the other half represent the audience and ask questions, raise issues, and express opinions.

competency Having sufficient knowledge, skill, and ability to carry out work to the required on-the-job standards.

computer-assisted instruction (CAI); computer-based learning (CBL); computer-based training (CBT) A series of highly structured, self-paced learning segments, presented by a computer, which processes the learner's responses and provides immediate feedback.

conditioning A subconscious response to a stimulus which a person reacts to without even thinking about it. Brainwashing is an extreme form of conditioning.

consensus Agreement by individuals or groups previously in conflict with each other.

continuum An uninterrupted series of gradual changes.

contract Self-directed course of study agreed upon by the learner and a facilitator based on a diagnosis of the learner's own needs and learning style.

credit A value assigned to a unit of learning which reflects the time and effort required to achieve its learning outcomes.

CRI (criterion-referenced instruction) Learner-controlled process in which new skills are broken down into specific objectives, each with its measurement criteria. Emphasis is on reaching required standards, not on the time taken to do so.

critical-incident technique (CIT) Flexible set of procedures for collecting and analyzing behavior, designed to provide information on the performance of a job or activity.

critique Analysis of the strengths and weaknesses of a specified activity and suggestions for improving it. Formalized feedback.

CSC (confrontation, search, and cope) Three-part experience in which the learner faces a problem or a need (confrontation), is responsible for seeking out a solution (search), and then applies it to the problem (cope).

culture The total attainments and learned behavior patterns of a training group forming a common culture group.

culture shock Bewilderment due to new customs, unknown expectations, a feeling of being conspicuous, different, and foreign.

debriefing A reporting back and sharing of experiences of what was learned from a challenging game, exercise, role-play, or situation.

Delphi technique Procedure for obtaining the pooled opinions or estimates of experts who do not meet; relies upon statistical averaging of individual judgments—a consensus-seeking technique. Usually carried out as a postal questionnaire.

dialectic The development of contradictions and their solutions as a way of advancing learning and thought.

didactic teaching Traditional approach to teaching, where the teacher is the authority.

diffusion The process by which innovative ideas spread over time.

discovery learning Learning through doing—also called *action learning* or *experiential learning.*

discussion group (buzz group) Two or more persons come together to talk about a topic of mutual concern. Experiences are shared, opinions expressed, alternatives discussed, and actions planned.

DPT (diagnosis, prescription, treatment) Learner's needs and/or weaknesses are uncovered (diagnosis) and a course of action or a plan of study is developed (prescription) which the learner follows to overcome the deficiency (treatment).

drill Repetitive, structured practice (written, oral, or physical) to reinforce learning.

dyad Two persons who share training exercises.

dynamics Energies and forces derived both from individuals and their interaction with one another and from the effects of these influences on behavior.

empower Authorize or delegate authority to a person or persons.

evaluation Objective assessment of strengths and weaknesses of particular training activities—usually aimed at providing feedback and suggesting improvements. May be ongoing, terminal (at completion), or some time after completion.

experiential learning Allowing the learner to learn from experience. Learning through doing. Also called *action learning* or *discovery learning.*

extension The process of extending technical service to clients.

extroversion Tendency to be outgoing and sociable, preferring to deal with people rather than ideas.

facilitator A trainer who allows students to assume responsibility for their own learning by guiding and encouraging them to achieve the planned results.

feasibility study A study of resources available to determine whether a project is practicable.

feedback A process in which knowledge of the results of a past performance leads to modification of a future performance.

fishbowl Also known as *clusters.* Technique in which some members of a class observe the activity of others and study interactions. Often groups reverse roles.

five M (5M) A problem-solving technique using the following headings: manpower, machinery, materials, methods, and money.

force field analysis A problem-solving technique in which the forces both favorable and unfavorable are examined.

forum Experts present diverse views but do not challenge one another, then the audience is given a chance to question and comment.

free recall Learners are asked to produce a list of things, as long as possible in the time allowed. (For example: Make a list of the annoying habits of bosses you have worked for.)

goal A terminal point in a plan or exercise; a desired achievement.

group dynamics Process of interaction of a group at work; study of forces interacting within a group.

handout Written or illustrative material given out before or after a lecture to provide detailed additional information. Often called a *take home*.

heterogeneous Of different kinds.

hierarchy A system of ranking any relationship of individuals, groups, or classes.

homogeneous Of the same kind.

homophily The degree to which pairs of individuals who interact are similar in certain attributes, such as social status.

icebreaker Exercise designed to relax trainees at the start of a course, to get them acquainted, and to get them involved in their training.

impact point The point where things happen.

in-basket exercise A simulated activity where a trainee is given an office in-basket containing a collection of memos, letters, and directives that pose problems. The trainee must set priorities, make decisions, and handle difficulties.

incident process Learners are presented with an incident which must be examined to produce other types of information. When enough facts are gained from the trainer, teams are formed to work out a solution to the problem.

induction training Training designed to introduce a new trainee into an organization.

inoculation Method of changing attitudes by exposing to weak, easily understood counterarguments rather than by presentation of favorable arguments.

instructional objective Statement laying down a set of instructions and a series of tests designed to show the extent to which the learner has profited from them.

intelligence quotient (IQ) Index comparing a person's performance on age-graded intelligence tests with their chronological age.

interactive modeling Learner observes model behavior and attempts to copy it until an acceptable standard is reached.

internalization An individual's complete acceptance of a social norm until it becomes the natural thing to do.

introspection Looking inward at one's attitudes, beliefs, values, perceptions, and behaviors.

introversion Tendency to be shy and to withdraw into oneself.

jargon Specialized terms used by various groups of a society, such as a trade or a profession.

job-instruction training On-the-job, routine-task training.

journaling Capturing in writing one's feelings, attitudes, and values. Used to give insight into trainees' feelings about their training.

KAP Knowledge, attitude, and practice.

KIS Keep it simple.

lateral thinking Ability to think in a nonconsecutive way and to link unrelated topics.

learning contract A plan to accomplish something as a result of a training experience.

learning yeast A motivational force that stimulates learning.

listening group Audience is divided into listening groups, each of which listens to a specific part or facet of a lecture or discussion. Later, groups report their findings to the audience.

live case A topical case study, or problem, presented to a training group as an exercise.

Machiavellianism Ability to manipulate people to get and keep political power.

MBO (management by objectives) An organization shares its goals with its managers, supervisors, and staff to help to achieve these goals.

mirroring Feedback technique used to demonstrate a person's body language. The person mirroring adopts the learner's postures and behavior. Used to show how words can often be inconsistent with body language.

mnemonic Word or collection of letters intended to help memory.

modeling Situation in which the learner observes and tries to copy model behavior.

module An independent learning unit.

mores The social norms that provide the moral standards of behavior of a group or society.

motivation An inner drive or impulse that causes a person to make the necessary effort to achieve.

networking Trainees keep in touch after a training program to support one another and share experiences, thus reinforcing their training.

nominal group technique A device to overcome shyness and prevent domination. Individuals work in each other's presence but do not interact. Their comments, written on cards, are shared among the group.

norm The commonly accepted form of social behavior.

objective A target to be achieved in response to a need. What is to be achieved? By what margin? By what standards? By when?

open-ended question A question that requires more than a "yes" or "no" for a reply. Used to draw the speaker out.

outputs Products or services generated by an activity in order to achieve projected objectives.

panel A group of usually three to five knowledgeable persons holding an orderly discussion on a set topic in front of an audience.

pecking order Informal ranking which determines who interacts with whom and under what circumstances.

peer-assisted learning Students act as both teacher and learner by switching roles.

peer group Informal social group, usually of the same socioeconomic level, education, age, or in a similar profession or job.

pilot training A training course that serves as a trial on a small scale before being adapted for large-scale use.

planned silence Quiet period in which to examine a problem for a possible solution or to think through views on a subject.

principle An important belief about a cause-and-effect relationship that applies anywhere and at all times.

programmed instruction Material presented in a variety of ways as a series of graduated steps—a form of self-paced learning.

psychodrama A real-life situation is acted in front of a group, which then discusses the implications of the performance.

quality circle An employee group which identifies and recommends ways to help resolve production and quality problems.

rapport A sympathetic and compatible relationship between two people.

rationalization A form of self-justification. A defense mechanism in which acceptable reasons for contact replace the real, but anxiety-arousing ones.

role-playing Acting out an improvised situation in front of an audience. Groups then discuss the implications of the performance.

self-actualization One's need to become all one is capable of becoming.

self-paced learning Learning at one's preferred pace, with built-in tests to ensure each test is mastered before new material is introduced.

semantics Study of the relationship between words and their meanings.

seminar A training method used to present ideas under the guidance of an expert or experts in the subject.

sensitivity training Improving trainee's skills in understanding the feelings and needs of others.

set A way of reacting to an event because of past experiences.

simulation Prepared situation which allows students to have an experience without incurring the normal risks.

simulation model Computer information-processing program designed to duplicate thought and other processes.

skit A short, rehearsed, humorous (often satirical) presentation, often used to promote group discussion.

smorgasbord training A number of training events carried on at the same time, with students free to attend their choice(s).

sociology The science which deals with humans in their relationships with each other.

stereotype Gross generalization based on narrow traits in common, but applied to all the members of a group, regardless of their differences.

strategy A combination of approaches and methods chosen or developed to reach a particular set of goals.

subliminal perception Visual stimuli presented at speeds above or below the threshold of awareness and recorded in the memory without going through the thinking, problem-solving, reasoning, or other normal processes.

symposium A series of short speeches by authorities covering various aspects of a subject—usually followed by questions and audience involvement.

synergy The total amount of effort or energy available to a group for a given purpose where the individuals' excitement stimulates the whole group.

target A precise statement of what one hopes to achieve within a given time. Targets are short-term results often derived from objectives.

team building Concept which uses various instructional techniques to build an effective work group.

teleconference An electronic get-together. A prearranged telephone or satellite-link conference involving groups of people in various locations or countries.

T-group A training method used to surface personal feelings between a pair with the hope of resolving deep-seated interpersonal problems.

think tank A group of people that generates ideas by means of a variety of strategies, such as brainstorming.

transaction analysis (TA) Method of analyzing the interaction (transaction) between two persons in relation to three mental stages (adulthood, parenthood, and childhood) of the respondent.

triad Group of three persons who share experiences, coaching, and plans.

validity The extent to which an assessment procedure measures the things it was designed to measure.

vignette A short segment of a film or video used to present a problem or a situation for discussion.

workshop A group in retreat from their workplace for hands-on training, to share common experiences, to plan, to study, to solve problems, and to extend their knowledge through discussion.

Index

OTHER BUSINESS ONE IRWIN TITLES OF INTEREST TO YOU:

A MANAGER'S GUIDE TO GLOBALIZATION
Six Keys to Success in a Changing World
Stephen H. Rhinesmith
Co-published by the American Society for Training and Development/Business One Irwin
Discover the six key skills needed to effectively compete in an increasingly internationally challenging environment. Rhinesmith shows you how to develop a corporate culture that allows your organization to adapt to a world of constant change.
ISBN: 1-55623-904-1

THE SALES MANAGER'S GUIDE TO TRAINING AND DEVELOPING YOUR TEAM
National Society of Sales Training Executives
This essential resource includes checklists to assist you in managing a staff; forms for training, planning, and evaluating performance; and a listing of additional sources of information. You'll discover how to train your sales staff for peak performance, conduct efficient and highly productive meetings, fairly evaluate performance, and lead the sales team to success.
ISBN: 1-55623-652-2

BUSTING BUREAUCRACY
How to Conquer Your Organization's Worst Enemy
Kenneth Johnston
You'll find a blueprint for unleashing organizational effectiveness while building an environment in which service and quality programs can thrive. Johnston shows you how to create a mission-based organization so that employees can focus on the actual goals of the company and not petty politics.
ISBN: 1-55623-878-9

FIRING ON ALL CYLINDERS
The Service/Quality System for High-Powered Corporate Performance
Jim Clemmer with Barry Sheehy and Achieve International/Zenger-Miller Associates
Improve service and quality within your organization! This authoritative, crisply written book outlines Achieve International's Service Quality System, which is used by dozens of public- and private-sector companies, such as American Express, IBM-Canada, Black & Decker, and many others.
ISBN: 1-55623-704-9

SURVIVE INFORMATION OVERLOAD
The 7 Best Ways to Manage Your Workload by Seeing the Big Picture
Kathryn Alesandrini
Survive the information onslaught and find the time you need to be more productive! Alesandrini gives you a step-by-step action plan to help you manage your workload without resorting to outdated time management practices.
ISBN: 1-55623-721-9

Available at Fine Bookstores and Libraries Everywhere.

Please note: Prices quoted are in U.S. currency and are subject to change without notice.